Beginner

+

Intermediate Guide to Free Motion Quilting

Table of Contents

Beginner's Guide to Free Motion Quilting

Book 2: Intermediate Guide to Free-Motion Quilting

Beginner's Guide to Free-Motion Quilting

Introduction

In this guide, we will look at all the necessary aspects, from the basics. You will find in-depth information on the tools you need, how to prepare your machine, choice of needles and threads, the use of stencils and markings, basting, adjusting tension, and preparing your own designs. You will only need to make practice a consistent companion.

Some people may find free-motion quilting a bit challenging, especially because you may not achieve the even and perfectly spaced stitches that come with the craft. Besides, things can also get ugly! You can have a mix of small and big stitches spaced as if they had an attitude of their own. In essence, free-motion quilting hands you the power to create as you go, make patterns, give life and beauty to the quilt, and ultimately own it. There is just one rule—there are no boundaries, the sky's the limit, and this is a hobby that is supposed to make you happy.

Take up the challenge and let us subdue free-motion quilting. Aside from fun, and the everyday purpose of quilts, do you know you can pass secret messages, express your mood, and show your feelings through them? African-American slaves used quilts hung in the open to pass messages. The quilts even included directions and maps. You see how much you can pour out into a quilt?

Let's get right into it and fill our days with joy,
control, beautiful quilts, and a sense of achievement!

Chapter One: Features of a Free-Motion Quilting Machine

Today, there is a wide variety of machines to choose from. Let us look at the key features you need to look for, irrespective of the size of your budget. You want a machine that makes quilting fun and smooth and not a frustrating affair. A machine that caters to the unique concepts of free-motion quilting.

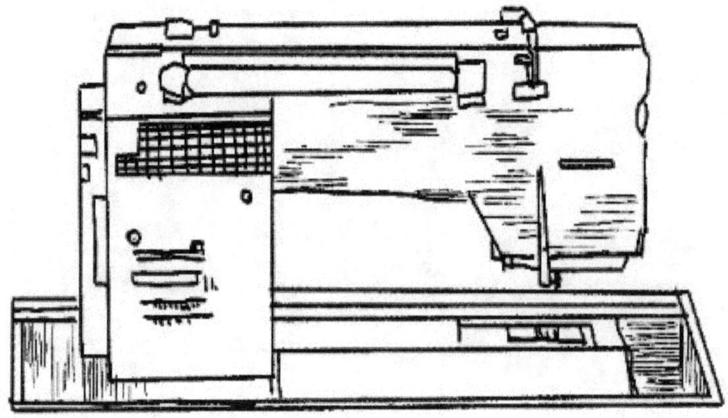

The basic requirements include:

- **Working space**—Space is crucial when doing free-motion quilting because you have to move the quilt easily. Therefore, it is necessary that your machine has a big throat. The machine's throat is the area behind the needle that it encloses, also referred to as the harp. A big throat ensures that you can easily handle the material without having to reroll, reposition, or fold the quilt, since you have space to stuff the material.

A long arm, again the machine's and not yours, is ideal for free-motion quilting. The arm refers to the distance between the needle and the machine's vertical part. A long machine arm allows for an easier creation of larger patterns. You can manoeuvre the fabric without much resistance. You are better off with a machine with a long arm and big throat for optimal working space.

- **Feed dog**—The term does not refer to a dog's dinner. In a sewing machine, feed dogs are metal-like ridges that begin from a hole on the throat and usually move as you sew. They grip the bottom fabric, helping it to pass through the machine and produce a stitch of high-quality. In most cases, sewing happens with feed dogs facing upwards and visible, but in the case of free-motion quilting, the feed dogs are lowered or covered.

  Lowering the feed dogs means that the machine does not grip the fabric's underside, giving you full control of the length and position of the stitches. In free-motion quilting, that is the ideal situation. Your choice of a machine must make it easy to move the feed. Most machines have a switch to lower the feed dogs, although older versions may have a cover. If your machine does not lower the feed dog, you can improvise by using playing cards or a piece of plastic as a cover. Whatever the feature of your machine, you need to have enough room to move the fabric around without the feed dog inhibiting your movement.

- **Presser foot pressure dial**—As a free-motion quilter, it is best to use a darning foot. They may differ depending on the machine, but generally, they have a base with a circular opening. A darning foot allows you to manoeuvre the fabric with ease and in any direction. With the clear sole, you have maximum visibility to quilt away happily.

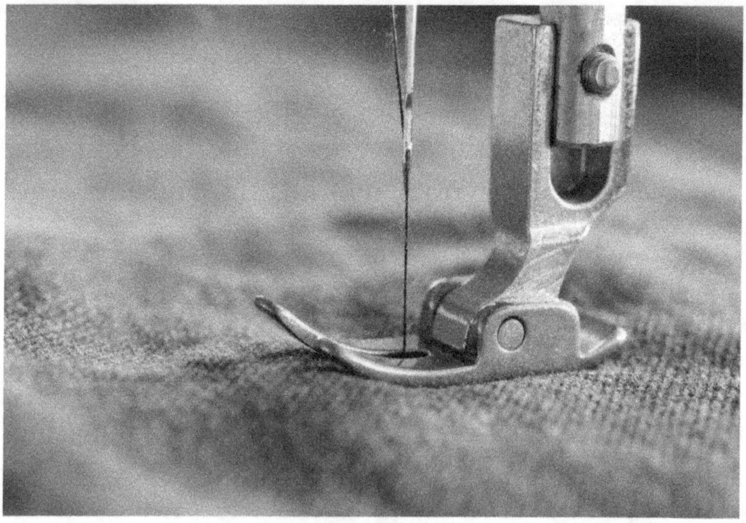

The foot pressure adjustment dial is important in setting the amount of pressure placed on the fabric by the pressure foot. Different fabrics require different amounts of pressure.

Nowadays, there are computerised stitch regulators that, once set, can produce consistent lengths of stitches during free-motion quilting, even with lowered feed dogs.

- **Knee lifter**—You will need a knee lifter to raise and lower your presser foot without using your hands. Your machine of choice should allow you to use your knee to raise and lower the presser foot. In free-motion quilting, you are the one in charge, and the hands play a crucial role in moving the fabric. You need those hands free and dedicated to the task at hand. Sometimes, it is not a knee press, but rather it might be implanted in your machine in the form of a button or heel press. If it's in a flywheel, it might be a bit bulky but it's doable.

- **Needle stop down function**—You need your needle to stop in your fabric every time you let the foot feed up. The needle stop down function helps the quilt from moving and shifting each time you stop sewing because the needle being down and in the fabric holds and prevents it from moving. You can then adjust your fabric or position it well without losing the pattern. As you choose a machine, this is an important feature to look for.

- **Half stitch**—This capability is important. You have to bring up a bobbin thread, which you will learn further along in this book.

Accessories

Now that you know the best features to look for in a free-motion quilting machine, you may want to know the extras. We all love something extra, and if you need evidence walk into a store and watch the items that come with something *extra* fly off the shelf. Even in quilting, it is always nice to have something that makes life more cheerful or eases things.

Although your machine has all the necessary features, there are a few items that you can add to make your quilting journey smooth and pleasant. You don't have to get them, but it would be beneficial to have them.

- **A free-motion quilting foot**—If you can only have one accessory, then have this one. A free-motion quilting foot does not impair your vision. You, therefore, can move the quilt freely and see your work clearly. There will be no guessing how the stitch looks or pulling it out to see. The good news is that you have choices; you can choose stable or hopping, metal or clear, closed or open. You may need to consult your machine's manual to find the right type.

However, there are generic feet available on the market, and you can always opt for one of those if you are unsatisfied.

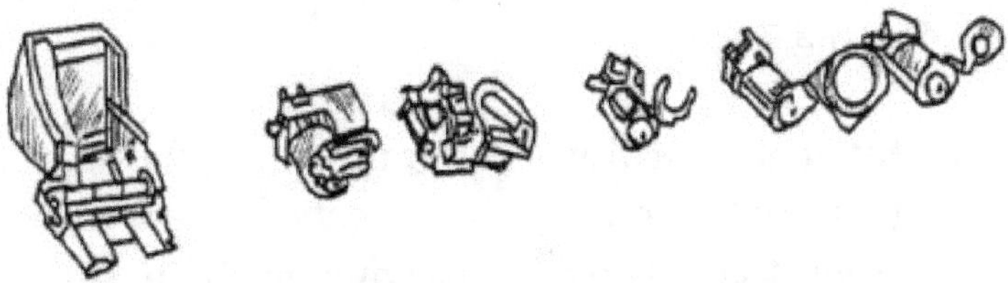

- **Extension table**—You want to work as comfortably as possible, and an extension table will do just that for you. The extension is a rectangular platform made of plastic that is designed to fit around your quilting machine securely. Its work is to extend your working surface to the height of the needle. You can therefore, easily support your quilt and free-motion quilt for longer without hand fatigue. Additionally, you can create nice shapes and designs because the quilt does not drag off the edge and can move smoothly. You may be excited to get this one, especially because of how it will allow you to work longer. However, before you do, you may want to ensure a correct fit. Your best bet is to find one made by your machine's manufacturer. Alternatively, you can look for a universal sewing table.

- **Walking foot**—Most quilters will own this piece of equipment, which is larger than the typical presser foot, and although more costly, it is worth the extra money. There is no assurance that your machine will come with one, so you may want to buy. The walking foot helps stitch all the layers together without any of them shifting.

- **Supreme slider**—You want your quilting to be smooth, and this slick sheet of plastic that clings to the bed of the sewing machine will come in handy. The plastic sheet creates a smooth surface covering for the machine's feed dogs, with a small rectangle cut left for the needle hole. If you have a domestic machine for free-motion quilting, then the supreme slider was created for you. It also peels off and on easily. The extra slick surface helps to move the quilt under the needle effortlessly, reduce fatigue, and spring some joy into free-motion quilting.

- **Quilting guide**—If you have a hard time keeping the surface of your quilt flat during free-motion quilting, then a quilting guide may be what you need. The guide is a weighted ring with a covering of a rubbery surface whose job is to grip the quilt. All you have to do is place it on the quilt, then work within the ring. Since the quilt is held flat by the ring, you will have a clear view of your work and only have to move the ring and not the quilt.

Chapter Summary

Your free-motion quilting machine needs to have various key features, such as an adequate working space, knee lifter, ability to lower the feed dogs, darning foot, and needle down function. You can add some accessories like a free-motion quilting foot, extension table, quilting guide, or supreme slider.

In the next chapter, you will learn about needles and threads, including how to choose the appropriate one for each project.

Chapter Two: Needles and Thread

The next step is to choose your needles and threads. You can be forgiven for thinking that these are not as important. The truth is that a thread is not just a thread, and neither is a needle universal. If you are to enjoy free-motion quilting, then you must know your needles and thread and use the appropriate one each time.

Thread

Looking at a quilt and its defined patterns, one thing that stands out is the thread because it is what brings out the pattern. Although most people may take the thread for granted, it plays a decorative role, in addition to binding the layers of the quilt together. In a way, the thread can help make or break your quilting job.

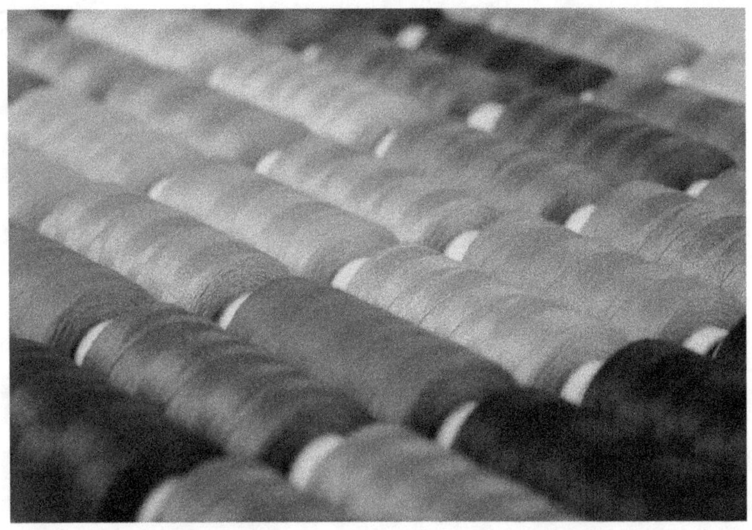

Many beginners think that cotton thread is the best and continually use it because of its pure form in terms of color and hue. However, the market today has a wide variety and you can choose what goes best with your fabric. When starting, you can use a lightweight, fine thread for free-motion quilting like thin cotton. A cotton thread of 50 weight is ideal, as it has enough strength to keep it from breaking and easily keeps the right tension to give even stitches. Using a thin cotton thread in both the top and bobbin balances the tension. However, you can vary the thread by using different weights.

Weight of the Thread

You will come across a reference to the weight of the thread in this guide. Do not bother buying a scale for that purpose. The weight of the thread, usually abbreviated as "wt," simply refers to its thinness and fineness. The higher the number, the finer it is. If you find yourself thinking it should be the opposite, you are not alone. To be clear, a thread weight of 80 means a thinner thread, whereas 30wt is much thicker.

Thread Tex

Tex refers to the density of the thread's fibers, usually measured in grams per 1000 meters. When the tex is larger, the thread is heavier. Note that tex is more common in Canada and Europe.

Denier

Denier, also abbreviated as "d," is the unit of yarn fineness that is equivalent to the fineness of one gram for every 9000 meters. Therefore, a 150-denier yarn is not as fine as a 100-denier yarn. The higher the denier, the thicker the thread. Note that not all countries use Denier.

Thread Material

As mentioned earlier, thread no longer comes in cotton only. Today, there is an entire world of threads out there, all waiting for you to discover and behold their different personalities. Yes, they do come with different attitudes. Some are temperamental and will snap at any extra pull,some are strong and will take in more tension, and yet others are beautiful and take the center stage. There are even combinations that offer a mix of characters. Let us look at some of the

most common thread materials used in free-motion
quilting.

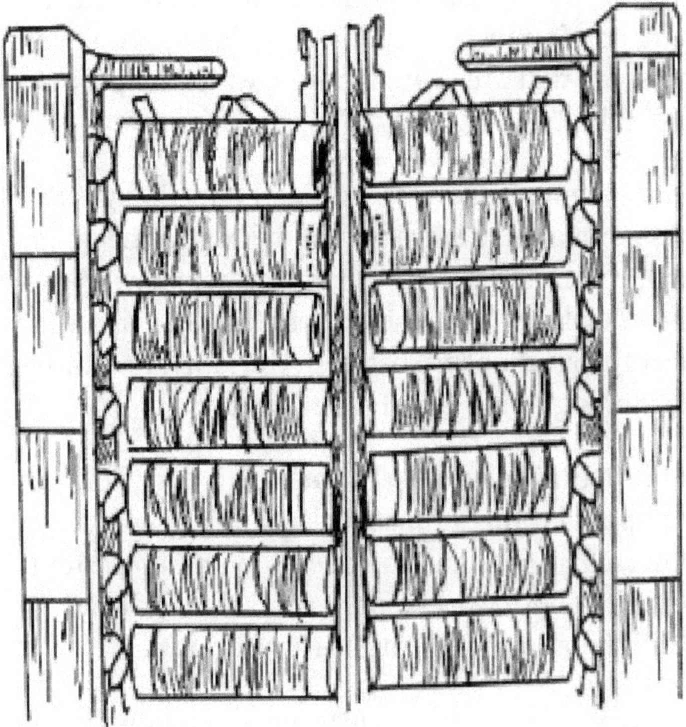

Common Thread Materials

Cotton—Cotton threads are some of the most
commonly used. The cotton plant is spun to produce a
cotton thread that is ideal for not only quilting, but
also other sewing projects. Cotton thread is both
resilient and versatile.

Nylon—Nylon thread is renowned for its
strength, but it cannot withstand the heat. Being a

synthetic elastic, the nylon thread melts at high temperatures.

Linen—The thread originates from the linen plant, and in most cases, it is spun heavy. You may find some that are coated in wax, which helps improve its durability.

Polyester—Polyester is synthetic, though it still does not match the strength of nylon. On the other hand, it is much stronger than cotton and can boast much flexibility and resilience to the many issues that affect the relationship between the fabric and thread-like melting, linting, and shrinking.

Cotton/Polyester blend—This is one of the more popular thread materials, widely used by quilters. The combination of cotton and polyester has the best of both worlds; polyester's strength and flexibility, along with cotton's appearance.

Silk—You may have learned about how silk is fine, and that is true. Silk thread is fine, but do not mistake its look for weakness. Packed in its fine strands is strength. Silkworms are the ones tasked with providing us with this high-sheen thread that radiates class. Most people use it for detailing because of its thinness.

Rayon—Like polyester and nylon, rayon is synthetic and mainly used in embroidery. What lets this thread down is its vulnerability to color fading, either from washing or over time.

Wool—Nearly everyone knows about wool and its heaviness. We tend to associate wool with warmth and not smoothness.

Types of Thread

You may have heard of metallic thread and wondered how it fits into a metallic needle. You most likely heard of a few types of thread-like bobbins and embroidery. The world of threads is deep, and in this guide, we will only scratch the surface looking at some of the common ones used in quilting. Since this is the beginning, feel free to keep delving deeper and trying out different types.

Bobbin—The bobbin thread is thin. It is embroidery that comes pre-wound and sold in large quantities that are spun on cones or in regular spools. All you have to do is pop on your machine if it uses bobbin.

All-purpose—If you have no idea what thread to use or are unsure, then the all-purpose has your back. Usually cotton—or a blend of cotton, the all-purpose is suitable for most free-motion quilting projects not unless you want a particularly thicker or thinner thread.

Metallic or Decorative—If you are looking for a thread with a bit of shine, then this is the thread for you. Nowadays, the metallic thread has gained popularity for its ability to throw the dull out of the window. The thread is called metallic because it has a coating of a thin layer of metallic texture, glitter, or color on the thread strands. At times, the thread may have all: color, texture, and glitter.

Water-soluble—Some threads disintegrate in water and are mainly temporary. You want to use such a thread during the basting of quilts or hold pieces together for a while. With this thread, after the purpose is done, you do not need to pick out the stitches you put in water, since they will have disappeared! Of course, this is not desirable for free-motion quilting. Here, stitches matter; in fact, they have a strong voice and make decisions on how the final project will turn out.

Quilting—You cannot use water-soluble thread, but you can use quilting thread, which is typically made of polyester, cotton, or a blend of both. The good news is that quilting thread is ideal for both hand and machine quilting. Don't relax too much though; although it may work for most projects and people, some may need to find something more specific.

Fusible—Mainly used in binding and applique, fusible thread, as the name implies, fuses anything that is in contact with it when heated. Some people use an iron to make the fuse. If you do not intend to make a fuse, you should avoid ironing this type of thread.

Embroidery—The choice is wide; it could be made of polyester, silk, rayon, or cotton. You can tell from its name that it specializes in embroidering, either by machine or hand. Embroidery threads come in small skeins and a myriad of colors.

Choice of Thread

With threads, you have to be open to experimenting. The same combination of threads may work beautifully on one piece, but border on the disaster on another. You should be willing to experiment beforehand, looking at the outcome of different threads on the type of fabric you intend to use for your project before deciding what is best. Once you have made your choice, you can then begin working on your quilt.

To start you off, here are some tips that can help you choose the appropriate thread:

- If you are looking for a star-of-the-party kind of quilt—one that is noticeable, attractive, and not easy to ignore—then you need to choose a thread of a heavier weight. 30, 40, or 50 is ideal.

- For your thread to blend well with the top of your quilt and have a great overall texture, it is best to make your thread finer, like 80 or 100.

- Choose a color that contrasts with your quilt top to make your project pop.

- Know your machine intimately, if possible. Some machines do well with certain threads. For example, the bobbin thread is suitable for machines with bobbins. Manufacturers make some threads specifically for certain machines.

- Read your machine's guidelines and instructions well, so you can tell if it allows for thread with either medium or heavy weight.

Needles

For many of us, we may use the same sewing kit for years. Why fix what is broken? Many quilters face the same dilemma. Some start each project with a new sharp needle, whereas some use theirs until it does not work anymore—either blunt or broken.

Many beginners get confused by the wide range of needles available on the market today. If you are one of them, you are not alone. Many quilters find needle selection to be a daunting task, with many of them opting to use whatever is in the sewing machine. There are simple guidelines you can follow to ease the process and ensure that the needle makes the quilting process enjoyable and effective.

1. **The choice of a needle depends on the weight of the preferred thread**—The two work jointly, and hence should be a match. As a guideline, a 40 weight thread pairs well with a needle of size 75. If you choose a heavier thread, you should increase your needle size.

The lighter your thread, the smaller your needle.

2. **Choose a needle by type of fabric and type of thread**—For example, a metallic thread goes with the metallic needle. It has a special layer of Teflon, which cuts down any generated heat. Choosing a needle based on the type of thread or fabric can get complicated. The needle may work for the thread and not the fabric, or vice versa. When choosing a needle in such a scenario, you can consider the following:

   - **Type of thread**—When using a specialty thread, you should opt for an embroidery needle or topstitch because their eyes are large. Choose your thread first, then look at compatible options.

   - **Type of needlepoint**—Is a sharp needlepoint ideal or one that is slightly rounded? A sharp needlepoint penetrates fabrics that have a high thread count like batik or those with coated designs. However, the penetration leaves the fabric with micro-tears. Topstitch and microtex are some examples of sharp needles.

   - Using a slightly rounded needle point will allow for stitching between the fibers of the thread without damaging the fiber. If this is a better fit for your free-motion quilting project, then you could choose a quilting, embroidery, or universal needle. If you belong to a group that is not very enthusiastic about changing the machine needle, then rounded needles can offer you some great results.

Your choice of needle will depend on the fabric. As we have seen, you cannot use a rounded needlepoint for fabrics like batik. Once you have determined the type to use, you can choose the size to use, as per your thread.

If you are working with a tight budget, then a universal needle may be best. However, remember to keep the success of the entire project in mind and do not compromise for a few pennies. After all, the needle tends to be the cheapest part of any free-motion quilting exercise.

Again, there are no specific needles; you should always choose what to work with depending on the project. Different machines and fabrics should all influence your decision for needle type. You should always be open to experimentation.

As a rule of thumb, always have an extra sandwich of a quilt with you to try out your combination of needles and threads. You may want to keep noting down what you tried for each to avoid a situation where you find the match but cannot remember which needles or threads you used. Ensure that material used in this dummy quilt is the same one you intend to use for your project.

Chapter Summary

You need to keep in mind that:

- There are different kinds of thread, so take time to learn and explore them all.

- Your choice of thread will depend on the fabric you are working with; a heavier fabric needs a thicker thread.

- Understand your machine well; that way, you can choose the right thread for it.

- Your needle choice will also depend on the fabric and thread you are using. Ensure that your thread can easily fit in the needle, but not too loose that it keeps falling off.

Chapter Three: Stitching in a Ditch

Stitching in a ditch is a very tricky exercise and requires much constant practice. Still, you can learn how to master the process. In this chapter, I will teach you how to quilt on a ditch and doodle some designs to enhance its aesthetics. I will also take you through some doodle designs to up your stitching skills a bit. But before that, digest this simple guide on how to quilt on a ditch.

Required Materials

- A ditch to quilt on.

- Threads (dark color, or those that match your fabric).

- Needle (based on your threads).

- Gloves (if necessary).

- A pair of scissors.

- Walking foot.

Instructions

Step 1. Ready the ditch for quilting.

Step 2. Needle and thread the quilting machine.

Step 3. Change machine foot from default to walking foot; its feeding dog will help you quilt in a straight line.

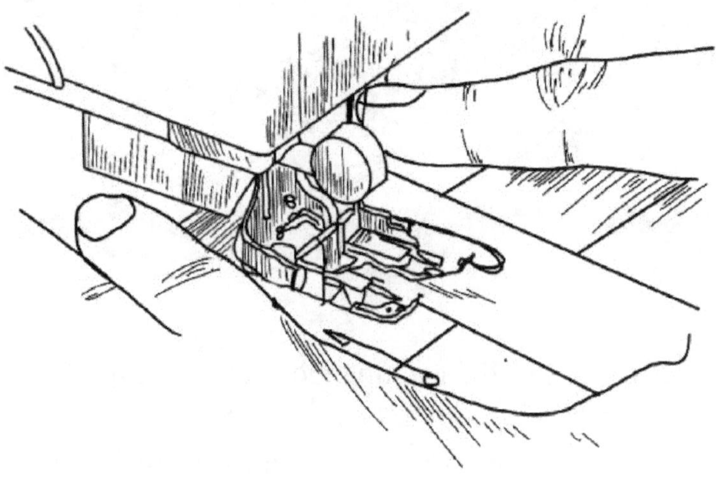

Step 4. Arrange your ditch sandwich carefully to fix the first seam on the walking foot.

Step 5. Quilt from one part to the other, but in a straight line.

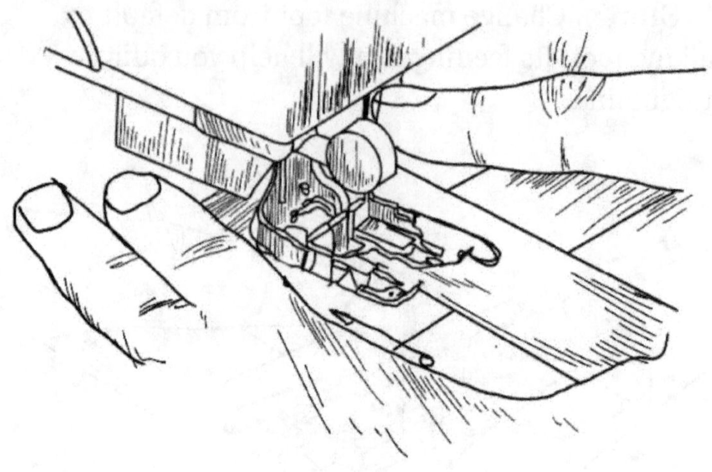

Step 6. Lift the walking foot, rotate the quilt counter clockwise, align the next seam accordingly, and lower the walking foot to jump stitch to another seam. Repeat the process until you finished quilting all the seams.

Step 7. Switch the foot back to free-motion mode, then quilt the sections within the blocks.

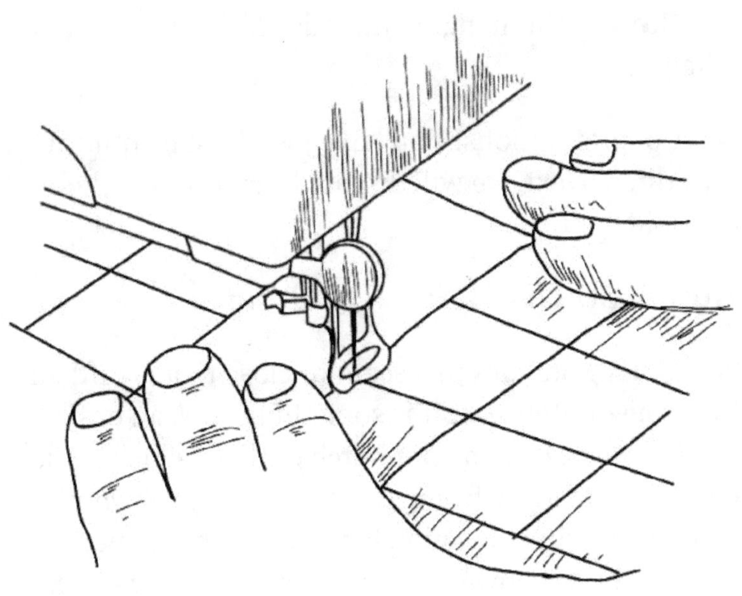

Step 8. Quilt seams in small sections of the blocks first. Then, doodle a few wavy-type designs in the ditches.

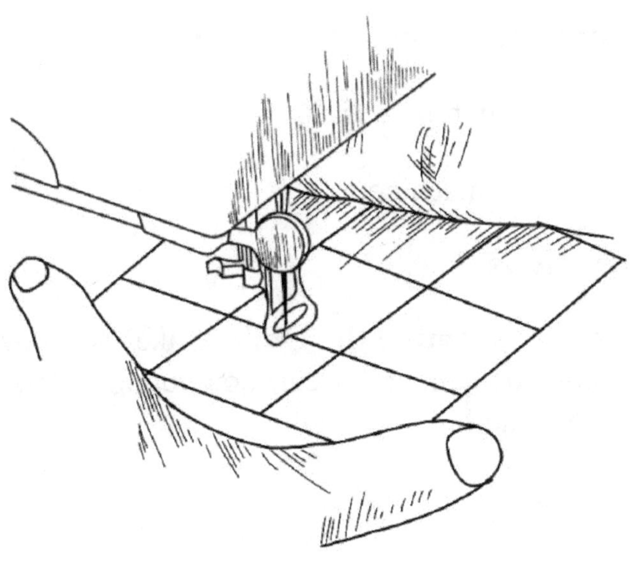

Step 9. Cut hanging threads off the jump stitches.

Congratulations! You have just finished quilting on a ditch. Next, we will discuss how you can stitch in the quilt.

How to Stitch in a Ditch Quilting

Placing stitches in a seam or close to it is difficult for some quilters, but it is something you can easily master. First, design your stitch outline, which could be ¼" or ⅛" away from your seam lines. So, whether you are working on a matching or a monofilament thread, you will always need to consider your stitch outline. Again, do away with thick threads that resemble a fishing line because they can mess up the whole show. Here is how you can run the stitch in a ditch quilting process.

Required Materials

- Two different fabrics.

- Sewing machine.

Instructions

Step 1. Examine the Quilt—Take your time examining the quilt and decide how you will press the seam allowances.

Step 2. Drop the Needle—Place the two fabrics on the seam and drop the sewing machine's needle on them, even as the bobbin thread hits the quilt.

Step 3. Place the Needle—Check the higher side of the seam to see where the allowance is pressed, but feel free to adjust the stitches by lowering the other side of the line. Tilt your needle down a bit to attain the best placement.

Step 4. Stitch on a Straight Line—Pull your fabrics apart a bit on both sides while you stitch in a straight line. Join the quilt to the end of the seam. Don't panic if your seams are inconsistent; it happens. Maintain a smooth stitch and keep the line straight.

Step 5. Add Quilting Motifs—You can add additional quilting motifs at this point, especially if your quilt has large patches. Should you need to add quilting motifs, read the instructions on your quilt batting before sewing them.

How to Make Bias Tape

Bias tape is an advanced and time-consuming stitch in a ditch design. Still, it is one design you'll love to do because you can tailor it to match the color of your fabric. Again, the bias tape is cost-friendly. Here, I will teach you how to create a unique bias tape through the piercing method.

Required Materials

- A piece of fabric.

- Half-inch clover bias tape maker.

Instructions

Step 1. Cut Your Fabric into Rectangular Tapes—Multiply the length of your fabric by its width. Divide the result by the width of the strips you need to get the estimated number of possible tapes from the fabric.

Step 2. Form the Bias—Gently fold the fabric to align the edges and form a triangle. Press the fold a bit to show a pressed line, also known as bias grain.

Step 3. Mark off Strip Lines—Ensure the width of your strips doubles that of the bias tape. The width will be shortened around the corner of the bias.

Step 4. Cut out the Strips and tug the strips a bit to stretch them.

Step 5. Trim the edges of the strips to flatten them.

Step 6. Join the right sides of two strips and sew them diagonally. Sew other small strips carefully and gradually until you have a long strip, but make sure everything turns to the same direction.

Step 7. Trim the edges of seam allowances and open them.

Step 8. Press the metal bar on the bias tape marker gently to feed the strip evenly.

Here is your single-fold bias. Feel free to fold it in half to make it a double-fold bias.

How to Make Bind Quilts

There is quilting, and then there is binding Follow these simple steps to bind your quilts.

Step 1. Cut Your Binding Strips—Add the width and length of your quilt and multiply the result by 2 to figure out the perimeter of your quilt. Add 10 inches, which would accommodate corners and seams. For example, here is how you would calculate your binding if your quilt was 52 by 70 inches:

$$52" + 52" + 70" + 70" + 10" = 254"$$

So, you will need 254 inches of fabric to cut your binding strips. Next, divide the measurement by 40 to get the exact number of strips to cut. Result here is 6.35", so cut 7 strips of fabric. Again, decide on the size of binding you want to make. Cut your strips 2¼" wide if you want the front and back to be ¼".

Step 2. Sew the Binding across its Length— Join two right strips at a 90-degree angle, but sew them diagonally at a 45-degree angle. Feel free to draw a diagonal straight line from one end to another to aid the sewing exercise. However, if your fabric is solid, you'll have to pin or tape the right part of the fabric to avoid sewing the wrong side.

Step 3. Press the left side of the binding thoroughly to the end of its length.

Step 4. Join the Binding to the Quilt—Square off excess backing and batting from the quilt before you attach the binding. Although a large square ruler can be used to clean up the corners, a long, straight ruler will be fine for the sides. Run the binding along the edges of your quilt to prevent the seams from falling to the corners.

Step 5. Secure the Binding with Clips before you hand-stitch them.

Step 6. Hand-Stitch the Binding—Thread some needles to hand-stitch the binding and create a quilter's pattern. You can double the thread if you want the binding to last longer.

So, you now know to bind a quilt. You should work on several borders and corners to make more amazing and unique binds, as well.

How to Make a Waistband

Designing a waistband is no big deal once you understand the method we used to make the bias tape earlier. A waistband is very easy to make, and you can do it right there in your home. Just follow the steps here to design your own, home-made waistband.

Step 1. Stitch the Waistband—Carefully consider the seam allowance in the waistband pattern before you stitch the fabric. You will still need to join the right sides of the waistband to your skirt once you're set to run the stitching process.

Step 2. Press the Wrong (Left) Side to Make the Waistband Flat—Again, tilt the seam allowance on the waistband and press it between ¼ and ½ inches.

Step 3. Fold and Press the Waistband on the Wrong Side until the stitching line is covered fully. Pin the waistband until you start the stitching process.

Step 4. Stitch the Seam to the Skirt, but let it overlap a bit at the back. You can use your presser foot to stitch the seam to your skirts.

You can sew the seams with a decorative stitch if you want your stitching to be partially visible.

String Quilts

Use the string piercing method to make your string quilts. String piercing, being a free-form quilting style, does not require you to mark out a pattern. You only need to position your strips, sew the seam allowance, flip up the right side of the strip, and add another strip until you have designed your favorite string quilt. String quilt derived its name from strings—the fabric used to design it. You can definitely use your favorite fabric, but ensure the fabric is thick enough to conceal the string blocks. Should you want to sew strings on a printed fabric, flip the fabric to its wrong side. Remember that the right side houses the print.

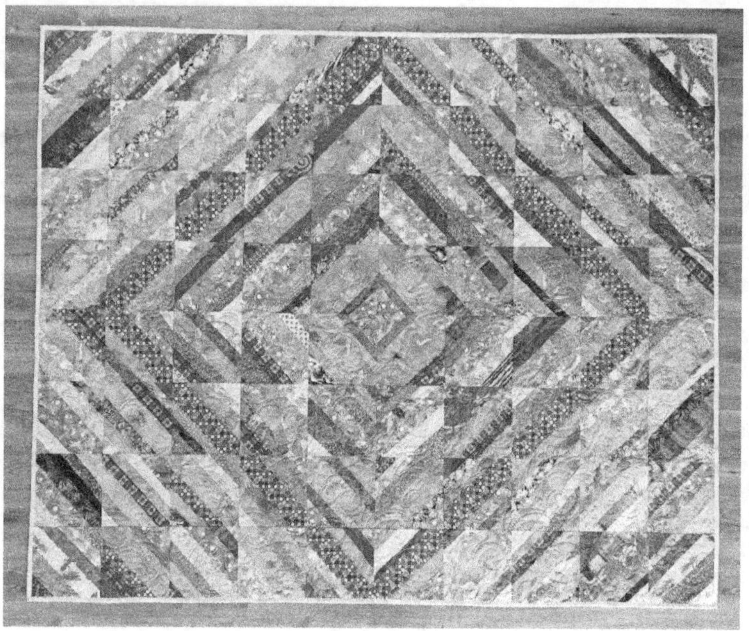

String Quilting Tricks

- Use a variety of strips of fabric for strings, not just straight strips. Cut both straight and angled edge strips.

- Care less about fabric grain placement, since the strips will stabilize the strings.

- Don't color match. Combine several colors and fabric styles to make your string quilt charming.

- Opt for quilting fabrics with several color values.

- Vary the widths of your strings. Strips for an 8" block or more should be between 1¼" and 2½" wide, whereas smaller blocks or miniatures should have narrower widths.

- Muslin and other pre-washed cotton fabric could be used as a foundation for the string quilt block.

- Consider beige or gray threads because they look great on every fabric, but feel free to use any thread you want.

How to Make a String Quilt

Step 1. Cut your fabric to a 9"×9" square.

Step 2. Position the fabric diagonally, right side up, and opt for a long string to cover it.

Step 3. Use straight pins to secure the string and lay another one down, with its right side facing down. Align the edges of the two strings, but let the second one stretch out a bit. Sew the aligned edges.

Step 4. Press the string to set the seam allowance.

Step 5. Flip out the right side of the string. Press and turn over the block to trim excess fabric or thread.

Step 6. Join another string, but align its right edge with the first string's unsewn edge, and start sewing the ¼" seam allowance.

Step 7. Turn up the right side of the second string. Press and trim excess fabric and thread and continue to add other strings.

Step 8. Iron-press the string quilt.

Hand Quilting

Handcrafted quilts are gorgeous and unique, and you can create them without sewing machines. People often ask for these quilts because they appear tender, beautiful, and natural. To design these natural quilts, you only need a few simple guides. After we go through the process, you'll be fine to start making your own handcrafted quilts.

Required Materials

- A pair of scissors.

- An iron.

- "Between" needles (short needles with small eyes).

- Quilt frame or hoop.

- Cotton threads.

- Safety pins.

Instructions

Step 1. Arrange and Baste Your Quilt Sandwich—Press the top of your quilt to open and flatten the seams. Face down, spread the quilt on a clean surface and tape or pin its edges firmly to the surface.

Place the batting over the quilt, but make sure it's spread on the quilt evenly. Also, bumps and wrinkles on the batting must be eliminated. Lay the quilt face-up on the batting and press the quilt back to split the fabric into three layers.

Pin the three layers from the middle of the quilt downward. Be sure the quilt is smooth and free of wrinkles, and you may want to hold them with safety pins. Make sure the space between the two pins is less than four inches.

You can use large stitches to hold the layers, but the space between two stitch lines must not exceed four inches. Trim the batting and backing on the edge a bit to keep them under two inches.

Step 2. Place the Quilt in the Hoop or Frame—Quilt the middle section before you deal with the edges to align the layers. Gently pull the quilt to prevent overstretching the fabric. You might pull the fabric out of shape if you do not handle the quilt with care.

Step 3. Thread the Needle—Avoid tangled threads if you want to speed up the process. Instead, start with 18" thread. As soon as you thread your needle, tie a knot at the end of the thread and trim it. Stitch the batting and quilt top from the top downward, but don't go near the backing. Opt for any thread you want, but make sure the color of the thread matches your fabric.

Step 4. Begin Quilting—Make up-and-down stitching lines at even intervals on the fabric. Again, these lines should be straight and normal stitches. Per inch, feel free to make at least four stitches.

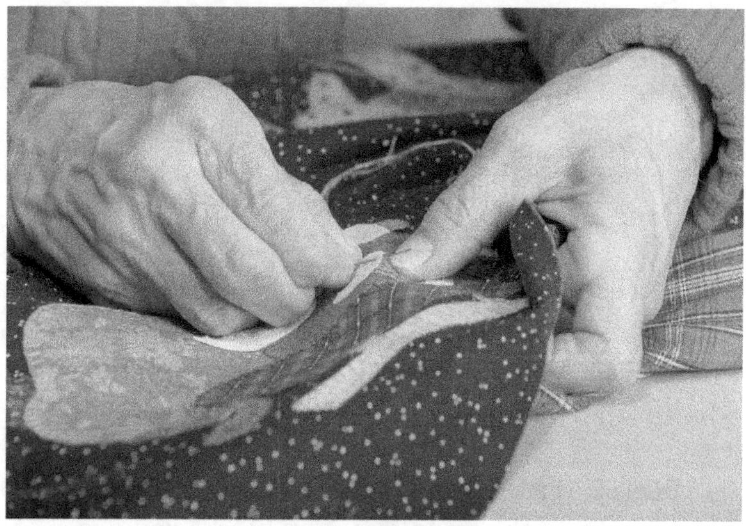

Stabilize the surface by placing one of your hands below the quilt sandwich while you are quilting. Carefully pull the needle through the quilt to avoid piercing your skin. Be mindful of the layout and make sure the stitches are smooth and neat.

Add more stitches to beautify the quilt, but make sure the stitches add value to the quilt.

Step 5. Add Final Touches—Take your time to examine the quilt to ensure that everything appears smooth and unique. Trim excess thread or fabric from the edges of the quilt before you join the binding.

Chapter Four:
Marking and Stencils

To Use a Stencil or Not?

You still need to remember the rule: practice and experiment. There are many quilters out there who make great free-motion quilts from patterns in their head. If you want to avoid the stencil and marker, then you need to work at committing the design into your head so thoroughly that you anticipate every move. With practice, this is possible. Besides, working with no markings will also reduce the beginner's pressure, thus helping remove jitters and avoid visible mistakes. There is something about following a line that makes some people's hands shake and vision a little blurry. If you can practice quilting without the lines, it would help reduce the pressure and allow your hand to follow your head.

Feel free to draw stencils on your projects but know that you don't need to follow the lines perfectly. Everything takes practice, and over time, you should be able to follow the lines seamlessly. After all, those lines marking the stencils are not permanent. Take control of your project and work at your pace, focusing on improving each time.

Use of Stencils

So, you have an idea of what patterns to quilt and are excited about starting? Well, before you even touch that quilt, consider drawing your masterpiece on a piece of paper to see what it would look like. However, if you are quite confident in your design, then you can draw it on the quilt itself. Whatever you choose, do not start stitching before you have drawn that design and loved the outcome.

One of the positives of using stencils is that you can use them even after basting the quilt. Sometimes, you may need to trace the chosen design onto the top of the quilt using a light box before basting. The choice of what to do lies in your hands. Remember that in free-motion quilting, you hold the control.

Your choice of a stencil can make your quilting work difficult. The best stencils for free-motion quilting are continuous lines. Occasionally, you could come across a stencil that calls for starting and stopping in different places. Although such a design is good for hand quilting, it may be challenging for machine quilting. By adding a curve or loop, it is still possible to create a continuous line, however, though it is easier to stitch without stopping and starting so often.

Marking

The market today offers many markers. You will need those marks to wash away and leave no trace of their existence on your quilt. Therefore, it is best to pick out your marker carefully. Although it may seem convenient to pick out anything that leaves a mark, you do not want to ruin your fabric or leave ugly marks.

Types of Markers

There are different types of markers that you can use to mark or transfer the design onto your quilt. These include:

1. **Chalk Pencil/Marker**—Also known as pen style chaco liner, though most people now refer to it as the chalk pen, marker, or pencil. Chalk remains a popular choice, and has been for a long time.

    You, however, need to be careful when using chalk; make sure to carry out a swatch test and don't press too hard into the fabric. You may have challenges washing the chalk off certain fabrics. Also, when using a chalk pen, it is best not to stack fabric together because the chalk may rub onto those other fabrics, causing smudges to appear on your carefully drawn lines. You need clear lines to ease your movement during quilting.

    You can opt for contrasting chalk pen colors to improve visibility.

2. **Quilt Pounce**—The quilt pounce is the "cool kid" of quilting markers. Here, you would use a pounce pad to transfer stencils onto the fabric. You run the pounce pad over the fabric to transfer it, much like the traditional ink and stamp. This saves you much time used in tracing patterns. The method is also simple and accurate.

3. **Water-Soluble Pencils**—As the name suggests, they dissolve in water. They are pretty stylish pencils that come in a wide selection of colors so you can choose what works well with your type of fabric.

    As a cautionary measure, it is important to test the marker over time, heat, and water to make sure you do not have a situation of resurrecting marked lines. On some occasions, marks may become visible after some time or with exposure to heat.

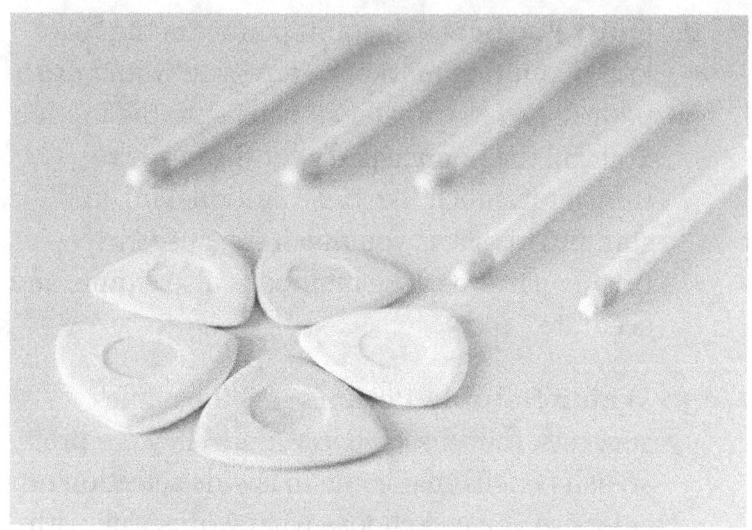

4. **Hera Marker**—Resembles a dull butter knife and is a favorite of many quilters. The Hera marker has a smooth finish and works by creating a crease in the quilt without snagging the fabric. There is no single mark left on the fabric, meaning that you need not worry about ruining it, or if it will wash off cleanly. The crease offers a subtle guideline for you to follow while quilting. If you want straight lines, you would simply pair it with a ruler and make the best straight lines without leaving marks on your beautiful fabric.

5. **Air and Water-Soluble Pens**—If you do not want to start washing off markings, then this is just what you need. The ink seems to disappear in thin air—literally. All you would do is mark, stitch, and the ink is gone! Although this option may be advantageous, it's likely not a good idea

if you have small children who need your attention or are easily distracted. By the time you turn back on your quilt, the markings could all be gone, and you would have to start from scratch.

6. **Graphite Pencil**—You can use a normal graphite pencil to mark your work, but you would have to be careful of leftover marks. If you have a heavy hand, you may want to steer away from a graphite pencil. The best way to use it is to make light marks. Always do a test; there are many instances when the pencil won't wash off, forcing you to invent a new pattern or make do with the ruined one.

7. **Frixion Erasable Pen**—Originally, this pen was not intended to be used by crafters or quilters, but as humans, we like to experiment. Since the ink "disappears," a few of us thought it would be a great tool for marking quilts. Despite the packaging calling it erasable, in reality, it is not erasable, but thermo-sensitive. The ink disappears when heated, and you should expect it to reappear when cooled. In terms of physics, matter doesn't exactly disappear; it merely changes form. This is the same concept.

   In some instances when used on a dark fabric, the lines may appear ghosted upon heat application. You need to be aware that Frixion pens contain permanent ink, so, although it may disappear, it will not wash out fully from your fabric.

With the many available options, it is best to keep this pen away from your quilts.

8. **Masking tape:** Yes, even a masking tape can get the markings done. There are quilting masking tapes that you can use to mark your patterns. If you do not have a marking tool, you can simply borrow some children's masking tape and get marking. Of course, it will not be pretty initially, but it will serve its purpose, all with no marks on your fabric.

    The added advantage is that you do not need an entire roll—you can use the same piece multiple times because it doesn't have to be super sticky; it just has to hold on to the fabric. Additionally, tape is thick enough to see, so you will not struggle with trying to guess on faint lines.

    However, as expected, it is difficult to do any other lines aside from straight ones. You will also have to discard a wad of tape by the end, even after re-using the pieces. In this sense, it is not an eco-friendly option.

What to Remember When Using Marking Tools

a) **Read and Follow the Manufacturer's Guidelines on Use**—Most times, we assume that we know how to do things. Who wouldn't know how to use a pen to trace out some stencils? Or with a ruler to draw a straight line? It sounds easy, but it is necessary to read the user instructions.

   Have you ever struggled to open food packaging, only for it to fly all over, with the packaging clearly saying where to cut? Some marking tools may need to be used in certain conditions, like temperature and in the absence of moisture. You could easily ruin your fabric and pour your work down the drain by not following the instructions labeled on the marking pen.

b) **Run a test**—You must do a test on every fabric you intend to use before the actual markings. If it says to wash, wash and see if the markings remain. That one minute of testing can save you from ruining an entire project, considering your investment in it. Delay your urge to get right into it and do a test. The **point** is to test first on a small piece.

c) **Press Lightly and Not Too Hard**—You can definitely press too hard on the fabric. The simple difference between pressing and applying too much pressure could result in damage. When using pencils or pens with fine tips, pressing too hard could cause holes in the fabric. If using markers, pressing too much could lead to bloating or lines so thick that you can stitch in a straight line. If your markers are dry, replace them; don't test your strength on the quilt.

Instead of marking the designs directly onto the fabric, you could use quilting paper to prevent exposing your quilt to chemicals from the markers.

Chapter Summary

In this chapter, we have looked at the use of stencils and markers and learned that:

- There are different markers available for use on the market, including water-soluble pens, chalks, graphite pencils, quilt pounce, and hera markers, among others

- Choose your marker according to your fabric.

- Always remember to test your marker to ensure it washes off.

- Opt for stencils with continuous lines for ease of free-motion quilting.

In the next chapter, you will learn how to prepare your machine for free-motion quilting.

Chapter Five: Preparation of Quilting Machine

Congratulations on getting here! You have all the basics at hand and have done shopping for your quilting material. If you have a new machine, now is the time to get rid of all those coverings and get her to work. If you pulled out your mother's grandmother's machine, dust it off and let us have fun quilting.

Having a machine is one thing and setting it up is another. Although you can get your quilting machine ready in a matter of a few minutes, it is important to ensure that you do it properly; otherwise, you subject yourself to frustration. For a beginner, the task may seem daunting, and you will probably be worried about getting things wrong. Relax—quilting is an activity that you should enjoy, so let us set up in simple steps.

How to Get Your Machine Ready

a) **Clean and Oil**—For new machines, this may not be necessary, but if the machine had been used before, you should clean and oil it. The stitch rate for quilting is quite high—about 1000 stitches per minute—often resulting in lint building up in the bobbin case. Frequent cleaning is necessary to keep your bobbin case free from loose thread and lint. You should also oil the hook to keep it in good working condition and make stitching easier.

Your machine comes with a brush for the cleaning task. Alternatively, you can use a toothbrush or stiff paint brush. Remove the bobbin case and brush it off on the inside, making sure to brush every inch, including the tension spring and ring. While you are at it, it is also a good time to inspect for burrs and sweep out the feed dog. Once clean, you can put one drop of clear quilting machine oil on the race. Remember to sew first on a waste piece of the cloth to absorb any excess oil before beginning a new project.

b) **Thread the Bobbin/Spool**—They say failing to plan is planning to fail. The case here could be true; you need to prepare adequately for free-motion quilting. Besides, once you get the hang of it, you will not want to stop. Thread your bobbins and prepare your spools. The key is to ensure that you have a considerable amount of thread to get you started. About three full bobbins are ideal for getting the project off the ground.

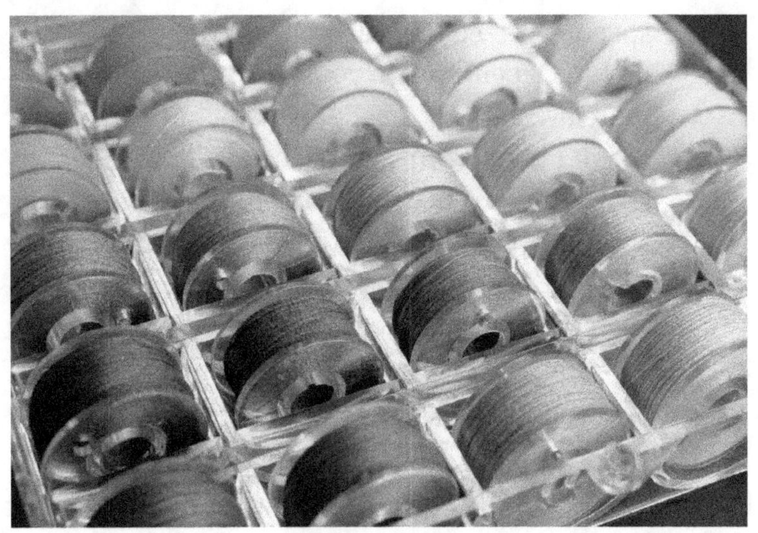

c) **Fasten a Straight-Stitch Plate**—Unlike the standard stitch plate, the straight stitch plate comes with a smaller opening that offers more support to the quilt and prevents it from getting pushed into the opening of the needle. It also creates beautiful quilting stitches.

d) **Put in a New Needle**—With your newly acquired knowledge on needles, choose whichever one matches your project. You can change the needle whenever you need to.

e) **The Quilting Foot**—If you opted to have a quilting foot, ensure that it is attached and ready for use. You will want to move your fabric freely and enjoy great visibility.

f) **Lower the Feed Dogs**—Since you are now in control of every stitch, its direction, and its speed, the feed dogs can take a well-deserved break. Depending on your machine's type, there are various mechanisms of lowering them. Follow your manual's instructions to lower the feed dogs, which will sometimes be as simple as pressing a button. Alternatively, you can set the stitch length to zero, which should keep the feed dogs in their original position so you can take charge.

g) Needle **Down**—When you set the needle down line of stitching when adjusting quilt position.

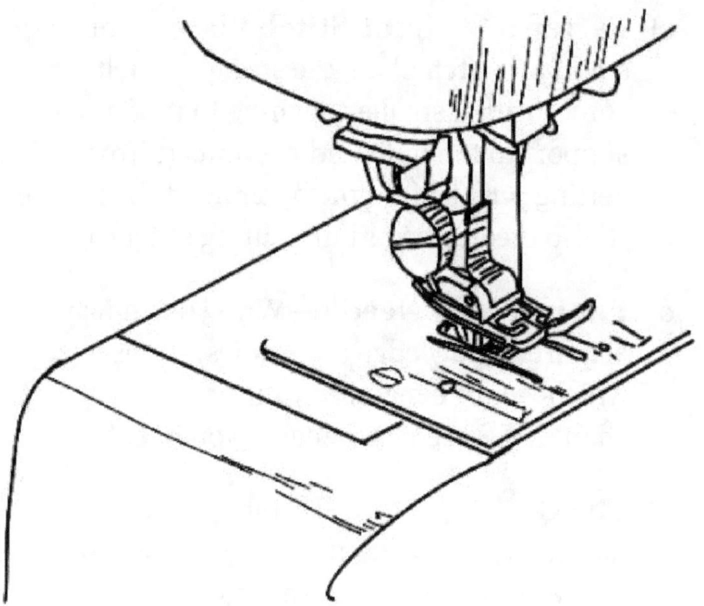

h) **Thread Your Machine**—Depending on your machine, the threading process may vary, but the basics will be similar. Refer to your

machine's user manual. Here, we will look at
the basics, and in case your machine needs
more, you can always refer to the instructions
that come with it or look online.

- Take the thread, and at the top of your
  machine, you will find a spool pin; that is
  where you will put your thread. Once you
  have put it in, the thread should be able roll
  and unfold easily when you pill it
  anticlockwise.

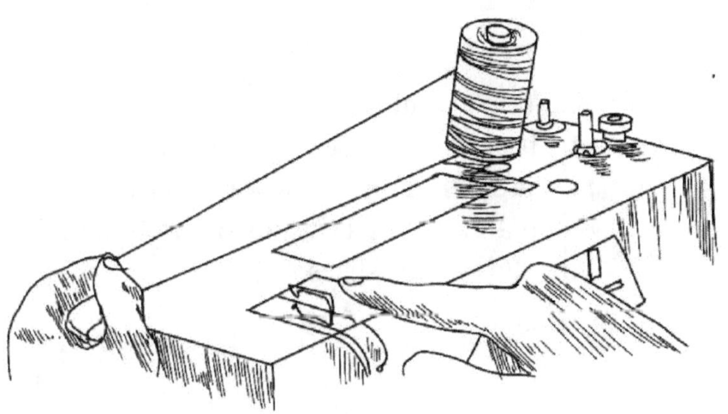

- Put the thread through the top loop and
  pull it down gently toward the tension loop.

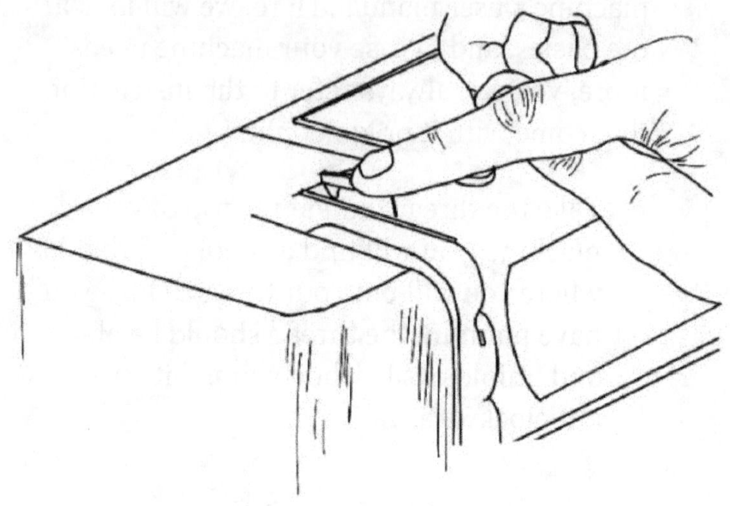

- You don't want the thread unfolding; use one hand to hold the spool in place as you pull it down. You can now press the thread down and through the cut-out to fit snugly into the tension discs.

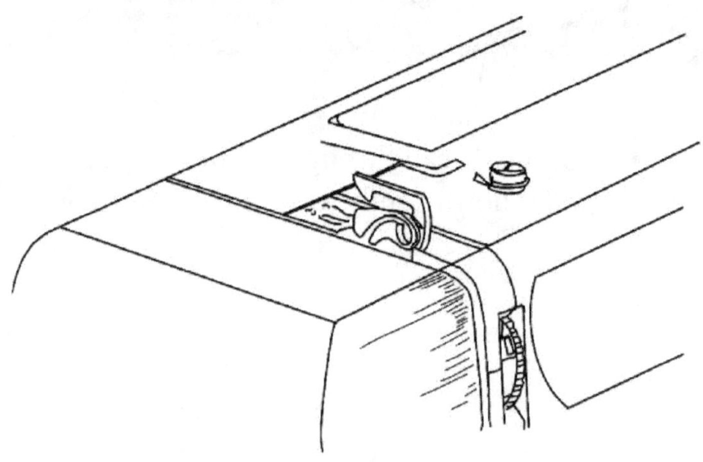

- Once secured, take it around the bottom of the next loop and pull it back up.

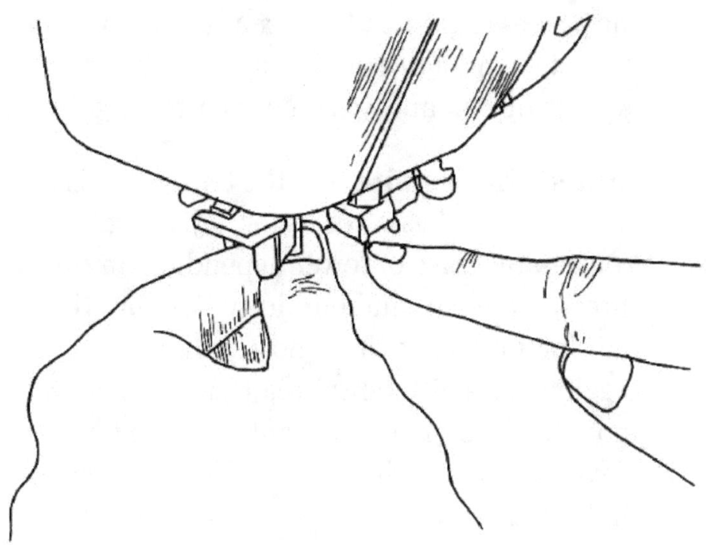

- Pass it through the notch hole, whose work is to pull the thread up and down. If you cannot find it, use your hand wheel by turning it toward you or your foot pedal to reveal it.

- Pill the thread through the cut-out again.

- Pass it through the hook situated above your needle.

- Insert the thread though the needle eye.

i) **Stitch a Sample**—Now is the time to test your machine to ensure everything is working together. Stitch a sample to test the thread tension, needle feel, and general workings of the machine. If there are any issues, go through the process again and adjust any step that you may have missed. That is why you have this guide; you can always come refer to it again.

j) **Adjust the Tension**—If the tension feels off, your machine has settings for adjusting that. You can increase or lower depending on the thread, patterns, and humidity. Free-motion quilting involves a little more pulling and tagging, uses different threads, and is generally more free. You may not want so much tension; play around with different tension settings to find the right one.

k) **All Set!**—The quilt is an empty canvas, and you an enthusiastic quilter. The time is now. Beginner jitters exist, but always remember that even the greatest quilters started somewhere and on a day like today. Embrace the "free" in free-motion quilting, make your patterns and mistakes, and enjoy the process.

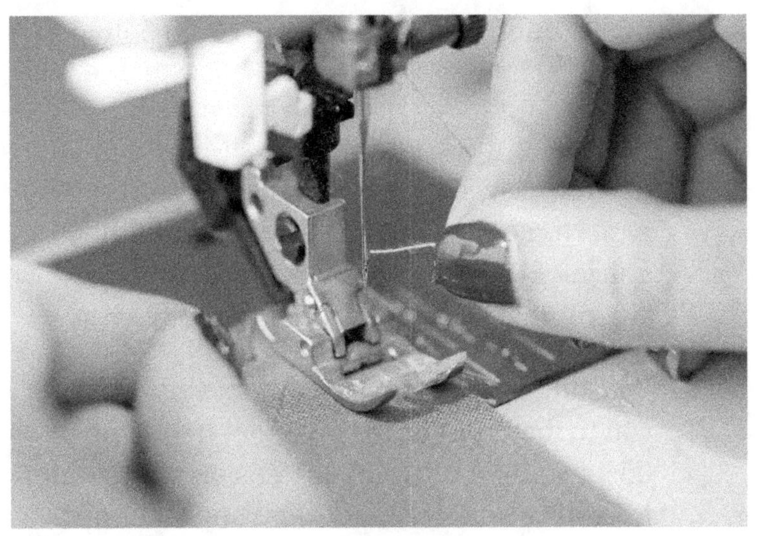

Placing Your Machine Right

You want maximum comfort when quilting. There is a high possibility that you will spend many hours on the activity because, once you get the hang of it, you may not want to stop. Therefore, you will need your machine positioned comfortably and in a way that prevents aches and minimizes mistakes. Here are some tips you should consider:

a) Place your machine on a large, flat table with a cut-out place to secure it. Ensure your machine is safe, secure, and not moving around, so you can quilt without any worries of the machine slipping, moving, or falling off. You also want the feeling of being grounded and in control.

b) Give your quilting table a back support, preferably from a wall. It is important to keep it in place and prevent your quilt from falling from the other side.

c) Place your workstation in a well-lit environment. Remember that you want those patterns coming out beautifully; visibility is crucial. Besides, working in a poorly lit environment will put a strain on your eyes.

d) Working in a clean environment will enable you to focus on the task without interruptions. Clean your working and extension tables well to remove smudge marks and any other dirt that may be there. Your quilt will slide smoothly on a clean surface and make your quilting more efficient.

e) Have a large working space and extend your working table, if needed. You will want a surface that fits the whole quilt without some of it hanging off the side. Even a small corner of the quilt hanging over the edge could mean an unnecessary pull and potentially bend the needle, making it thump into the throat plate and break. You can prevent such accidents by extending your work surface. You can put a table, bookcase, or any other surface that is of similar height adjacent to your machine to extend your working area.

Chapter Summary

Preparing your machine for quilting is a prerequisite condition for efficient and fun quilting. You need to ensure that:

- You clean and oil your machine, thread your bobbin, attach a stitch-plate, attach a quilting foot, put in a new needle, lower the feed dog, and thread the machine. Once ready, you need to adjust the tension and stitch a sample to make sure everything is working well.

- Place your machine in an environment that is conducive for quilting. Your machine should have the necessary support, and the environment should be well-lit and clean.

- Quilting is a relaxing and enjoyable activity, so create the right mood for it.

In the next chapter, you will learn how to make your quilt sandwich easily, including tips to help with your basting experience.

Chapter Six:
Baste Your Quilt

Quilting involves layering fabrics. Usually, there are mainly three layers: a woven top cloth, a layer of wadding or batting, and woven cloth at the back. The three layers would be sewn together through quilting. How you set up these layers is of utmost importance and determines how the final product will look .

Before you begin quilting, you have to place the layers correctly together and hold them together temporarily. The process is referred to as basting, and it is crucial in determining your outcome. Remember that all the layers have to be smooth and wrinkle-free. You have to make sure there are no puckers, since they restrict the flow of your quilt under the presser foot.

You need to ensure that you choose the right batting for your quilt because such also determines the general outlook and type of finishing. Let us choose our batting, and then we can baste.

Choosing the Batting

Have you seen all quilt waddings available on the market? It can be overwhelming. However, variety is the spice of life, and we should appreciate that we have the ability to choose. There are two main factors to consider when choosing a wadding: loft and fiber.

Loft—This simply implies the thickness or thinness of your batting. A low loft is thin, whereas a high loft would be thick. In other words, a low loft wadding would make a thinner quilt, whereas a high loft batting will give you a thicker comforter.

Fiber—Refers to the material that makes the quilt. In most cases, the batting is made of cotton, polyester, or a blend of cotton and polyester. Each of these materials has its advantages. For instance, polyester is lightweight, less expensive, and durable; however, it tends to shift if not quilted densely. Cotton, on the other hand, is light and breathable, offers the heaviest weight for batting, and is best for machine quilting. Your cotton batting will also wash well without pilling and shrink slightly. The cotton blend is usually made up of 80% cotton and 20% polyester. As it is not pure cotton, it is less-expensive and will not shrink as much.

The batting—mainly cotton and cotton blend— may come with scrim, which is a thin sheet of stabilizer on one or either side of the wadding that prevents separation or stretching of the fibers. Scrim makes the batting strong and stable, thus making your basting process easier.

Researching your batting is quite important. Manufacturers, in most cases, give guidelines on how far apart the stiches should be for each batting. Having this information is important to ensure that you make a quality quilt. You should always strive to adhere to the manufacturer's recommendations.

The Basting Process

Preparation is crucial. You can make your work easier by having all the items you need at hand. It will also save you time, since you won't be running around looking for items.

What to have at hand:

1. Top cover.

2. Bottom cover.

3. Batting.

4. Iron box.

5. General purpose masking tape.

6. Lint roller.

7. Dog pins.

8. Quick clip tool.

9. Safety Pins/spray baste.

Process of Basting

Step 1. Smoothen the Back Cover—Start by ironing the backing fabric. You want it to be smooth and without any wrinkles. Now that your quilt is ready for use, place it on a flat surface, face down. You can use your floor, an area with cleared out space, or even a large working table. Ensure there is enough room, so it is all spread out and taut *without* stretching.

Step 2. Hold it in Place—Using the masking tape, hold the back fabric in place by taping it on the surface. The surface has to be hard and flat to prevent it from moving or wrinkling. If you are using a smaller surface than you quilt, and it ends up hanging off the sides, you can use your dog pins to hold them in place. If possible, avoid a situation where your quilt has to fold.

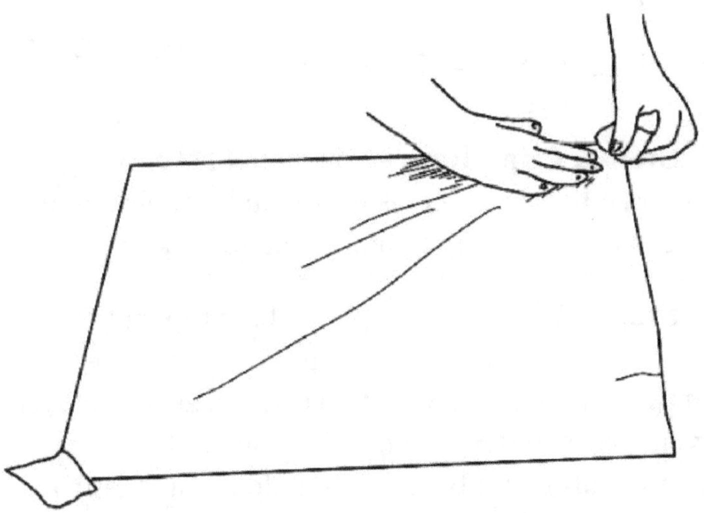

Step 3. Place Your Batting—Once your back quilt is well-placed, you can then place your batting. Lay down the batting carefully on top of the bottom cover and smoothen it. You can use a lint roller to remove any lint or threads that may be there. The

surface should be clean. You can then use your hands to smoothen the surface and get rid of any puckers.

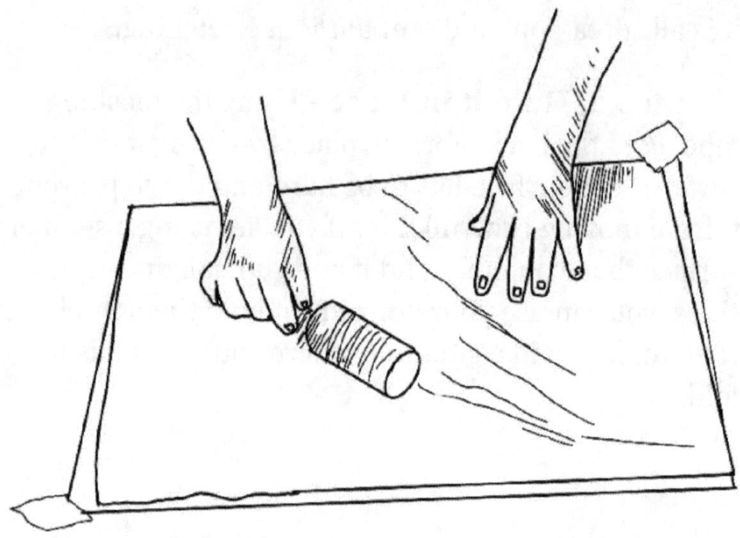

Step 4. Clip Them—You do not have to clip them together, but it helps to solemnize their union. You can use a dog clip to hold them together.

Step 5. Place the Top—Add the top quilt and smoothen it out so it fits well on the batting. Ensure that there are no wrinkles. You can add as many layers as you please, but remember that the more you add, the more difficult it becomes to hold them together. You should see batting material.

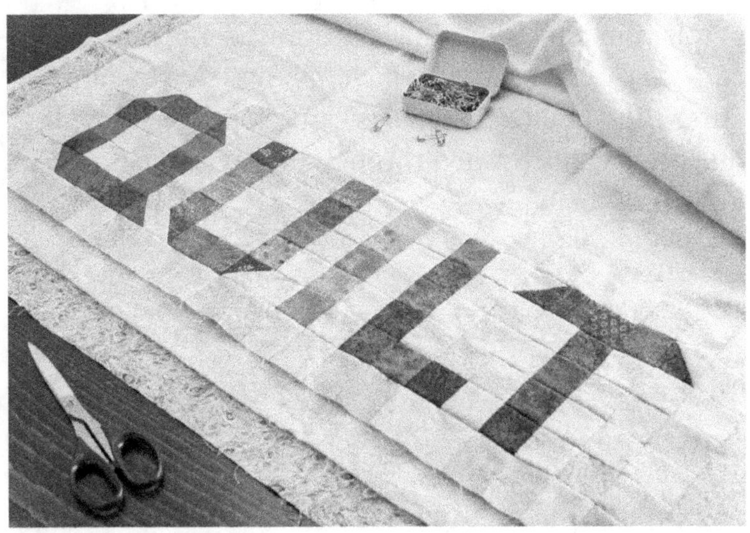

Step 6. Baste—The time is now to join the layers together. You can use a basting spray, which is available in stores. You must, however, ensure that what you get easily washes out. The use of basting spray calls for a well-ventilated room because it is harmful to breathe in. Unfortunately, it can also leave deposits on the floor that are hard to remove.

Alternatively, you can use basting pins. They are slightly curved, unlike regular safety pins, making it easy to pin through the three layers. Using the quick clip tool, insert safety pins to hold the layers together. The best way to do this is to start at the center and place pins every few inches as you move toward the edge. As you place the pins, you must be careful that you do not leave any pucker; you want a smooth finish, ready for quilting. Ensure that the edges also have pins in place.

If you don't like either the spray or the pins, you can use thread basting, which involves making large stitches by hand. Plastic tags can replace basting pins and are usually pushed through the layers using a gun-like tool.

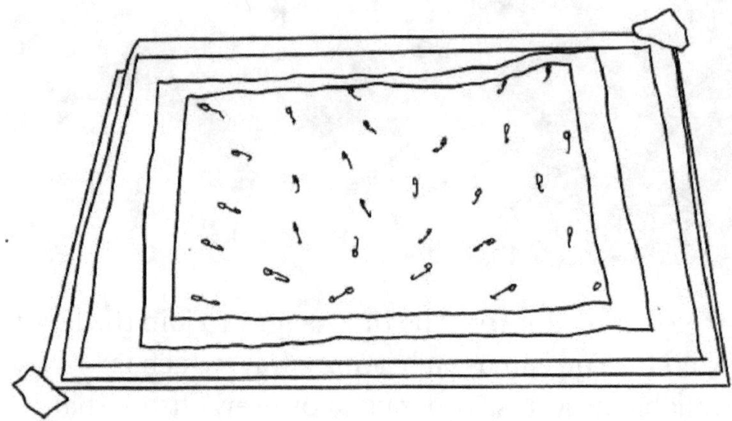

Step 7. Remove the Tape—When the pins are in place, remove the tape and check that everything is flat and tight. If you find puckers, excess fabric, or looseness, now is the time to fix it. You certainly will not like adjusting puckers after you start stitching. You can use a fabric with a busy pattern to help hide your beginner mistakes.

Basting Tips

Store Your Pins Open—We tend to close our pins instinctively, even safety pins. Resist the temptation to close all those pins and instead, store them in a box while open. Think about it—when you need to use the pins, you will have to open them, and when you remove them, they will be open. Isn't it better to leave them open? For safety's sake, you will need to keep the box closed and in a safe place; otherwise, leave the pins open. It will save you basting time during your next project.

Embrace the Kwik Klip—This simple wooden tool will save your hands much wear and tear when closing all those pins.

Use the Tiles—If you have a tiled floor, you can use the lines to keep your quilt centered and layers straight.

Don't Stretch the Fabric—The fabric needs to be taut but not stretched. If you stretch it, it will likely lose its shape, which is not what you want.

Cover Your Work Area—If you are using a basting spray, you need to cover the surface you are working on prior to application. The spray can get messy and leave residue. Besides, covering the surface will mean no need to clean up afterwards.

Iron the Fabric—Ironing the fabric will leave you with a smooth and wrinkle-free starting point that will make your basting work easier.

Chapter Summary

Basting is an important part of the quilting process, and although challenging for some, it gets better with practice. What you need to remember is:

- Your choice of batting is important; choose one that fits your purpose.

- Ensure that the fabric is taut without being stretched.

- Iron the fabric to prevent wrinkles.

- Smoothen as you baste to avoid puckering.

In the next chapter, you will start on your first stitches.

Chapter Seven: The First Stitches

As you switch on your machine, and take a seat with your basted quilt, you can be certain that from the first stitch, you cannot expect perfection, but you will at least continue to improve. Do not feel alone, overwhelmed, or intensely nervous—you are in safe hands. In this guide, we will walk through the first stitches to ensure that you do not go through unnecessary trial and error.

Choose your needle carefully and thread depending on your fabric. If you are a bit uncertain on how to do so, you can revisit chapter two of this guide. Remember that your choice of needle and thread is crucial in making your stitching easy and efficient. Before then, let us prepare adequately.

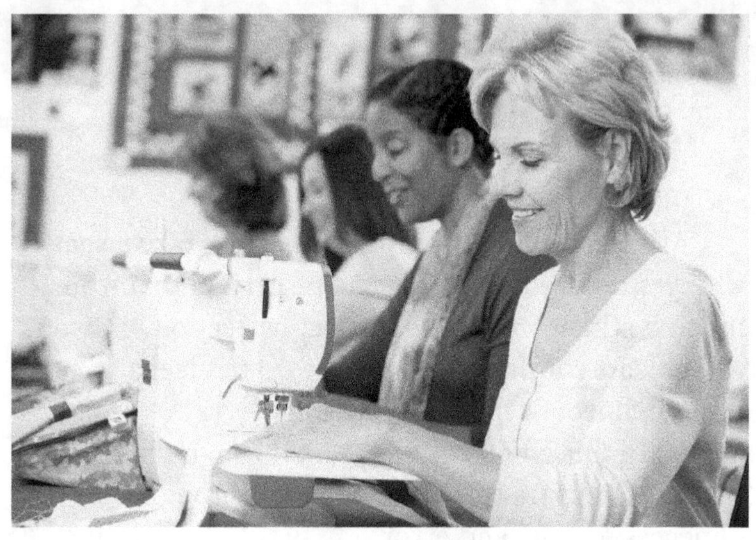

What to Keep in Mind

Large Working Area—If your project is big, then you will need a large working surface on your machine's rear and left sides to support the quilt's weight adequately. Failure to do so can result in your machine being pulled off by the weight of the quilt.

Roll Your Basted Quilt—Rolling your quilt will help make your work easier. After basting, spread your sandwich on the floor and roll from either side toward the center. You can secure the sides with bicycle clips or safety pins.

Start from the Center—When quilting, it is best to start stitching from the center and move toward the edges. This will help keep your sandwich intact and prevent puckers. Additionally, it is easier to balance the weight of the quilt this way.

Remove the Pins—If you basted using pins, remove them as you approach. Do not stitch over the pins, as it becomes harder to remove them and can interfere with your stitches. They can also result in accidents. The pins can cause your needle to break, and those fragments could end up in your eyes. Quilting is a fun activity, so don't turn it into a risky affair.

Use Rubber Finger Tips—If you have trouble moving the quilt around or have dry fingers, you can cover them with rubber finger tips, which are available in most stores that stock office supplies. Rubber finger tips will give you a better grip of the quilt, enabling you to move it easily.

Remember that your sewing speed combined with how fast you move the quilt will determine the length of your stitches.

Start Slow and Steady—The key to beautiful quilting is maintaining a steady machine speed and pairing that with smooth fabric movement.

What You Need

1. 2 threads (1 for needle, 1 for bobbin).

2. Needle, according to thread.

Steps

1. Check for disengaged feed dogs and an inserted darning foot. Your machine is ready for use,

but a minute or two of checking through it can save you much frustration and many mistakes. You have to make sure you disengage the feed dogs to gain control of the process. Also, make sure the darning foot is inserted and ready.

Once you are certain that everything else is on point, including having adequate thread, you are then ready to stitch.

2. Position your sandwich on top of the feed dogs, placing it in a way that the center of the quilt or spot you wish to stitch first lies directly under the needle. Ideally, you should ensure the quilt has a good balance and is well-supported as you begin. Place your hands on either side of the quilt—about two inches from the presser foot—and you can then use them to guide the quilt as you wish.

3. Adjust the tension by pulling the bobbin thread. You need the right tension from the start and may need to place the presser either up or down, depending on the level of tension you need.

4. Do a half stitch to pop the bobbin thread out.

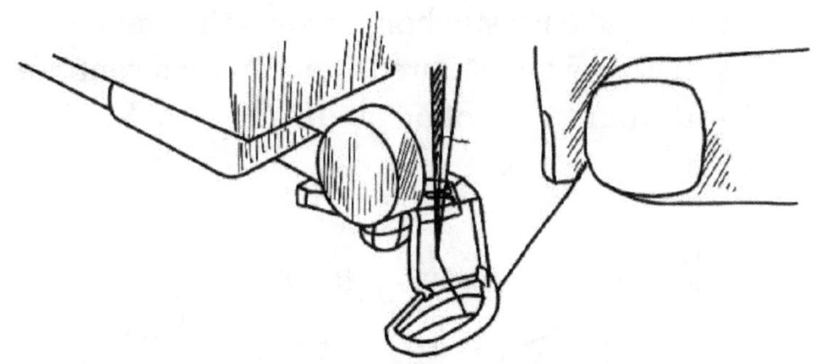

5. Hold both the bobbin thread and needle thread and pull them to maintain the tension. You want to ensure that you do not lose the tension you have already adjusted, and that you are all set to allow the needle and thread to meet the fabric.

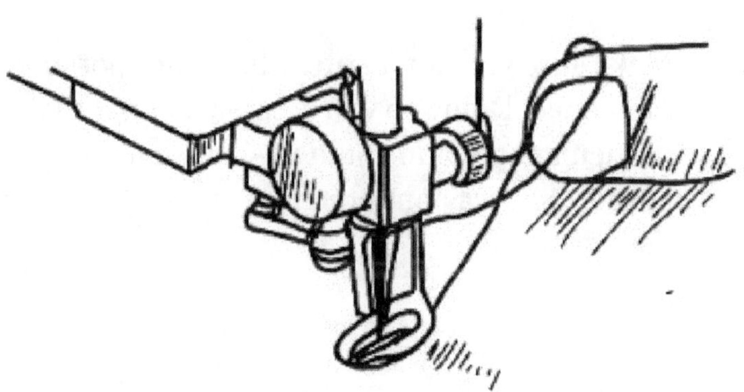

6. As you begin to stitch, remember that the first two stitches are very important. You have to secure them to prevent the subsequent work from coming off. To secure them, sew two stitches forward, then two stitches back. The

front and back stitching ensures that your stitches remain secured. You can then continue with your free-motion quilting.

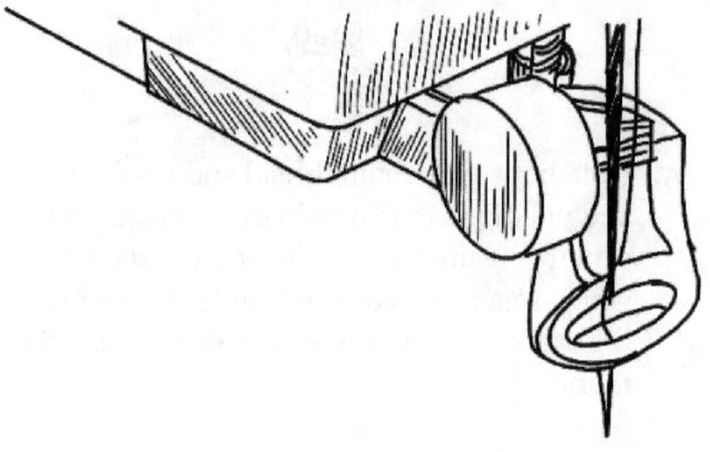

7. Make sure you don't stitch the same spot more than once. Doing so will create a knot at that particular spot and could possibly damage your fabric. On occasion though, you can stitch more than once.

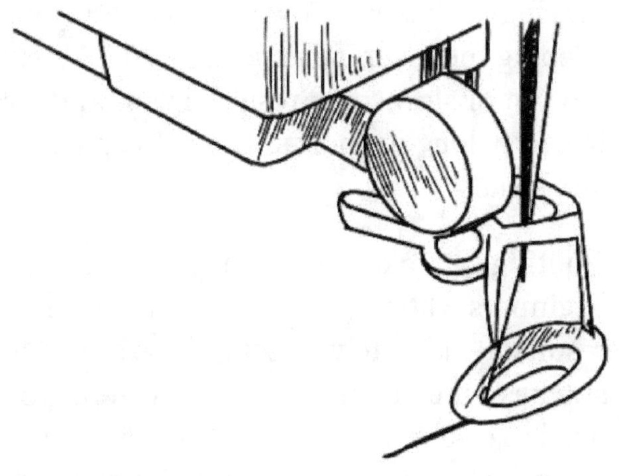

8. As you stitch, guide the fabric with both hands
    and move it so the needle traces the marked
    designs or lines. You will most likely not
    achieve perfection today, but keep up the right
    attitude and practice, and you will be proficient
    in no time.

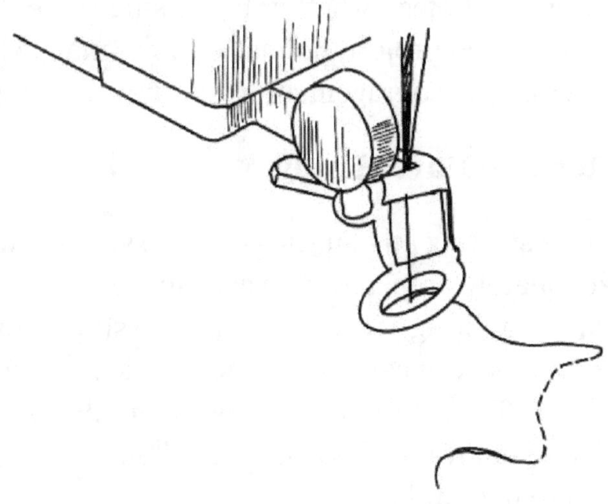

9. The secret to great free-motion quilting is moving your fabric slowly but smoothly while keeping the machine's speed steady. Moving too fast or slow could result in gaps and a mix of overly long or short stitches. Keep it slow and steady.

10. Quilting can take a toll on anyone, particularly beginners who may not be happy with the results. Be kind to yourself. These are your first stitches—much like a baby's first steps, you need to celebrate them, despite being a few and most likely not of high quality. Enjoy the lack of rules that come with free-motion quilting. You do not even need to follow any pattern; just let your imagination work for you and keep practicing.

11. Choose a small project to start with, like a pillowcase or table cloth. Everyone likes to finish a project, whether big or small. Seeing a completed project, no matter how small, will serve as encouragement to continue quilting.

Five Items to Have Handy

Before starting any quilting project, you will want to be adequately prepared. You certainly do not want to begin the quilting process and have to stop in the middle because you cannot cut your fabric into the desired size. To ensure the quilting experience is smooth and enjoyable, here are some items that you will need to have at hand.

1. Scissors

There are tons of different types of scissors available on the market. However, your key focus when looking for a pair of scissors for your quilting is on the sharpness of the blade and hand comfort. You need scissors that you can use without developing sore hands and ones that fit your hand well. While looking at the blade sharpness, you also have to keep in mind your environment. Blades made of stainless steel will not maintain a sharp edge for a long time but will resist rusting. On the other hand, high-carbon steel blades, although they do not offer good rust resistance, will keep a sharp edge.

If you do not buy any other scissors, you will definitely have to get some professional fabric scissors. Using all-purpose scissors could leave you with frayed edges or jagged cuts and very tired hands. The task can become a nightmare when you need to cut curves.

Ideally, you should have at least a high-quality pair of shears to use with long cuts; for the small cuts, you will want a good pair of scissors. With the two, you can focus on the creative process instead of the frustration. For ease of identification, scissors are short in size, usually with a total length of no more than ten inches. Shears are longer with a length of over ten inches. Most quilters opt for 12-inch shears, which are ideal for cutting long lengths of material and offer long, straight cuts.

A fabric scissors helps to easily snip the fabric. They mostly come with a curve handle, which improves the accuracy when cutting on flat surfaces. The pointed tips help with precision. A key tip to maintaining the sharpness of the blade is to avoid using the scissors on anything else other than your fabric.

2. Needles

You definitely know that you need a needle, and you have to choose one carefully according to the thread you are using and fabric you intend to stitch. However, what you may not know is that you need to have more needles available and not at the store, but within reach. Accidents happen, needles break, some become blunt faster than you expected, and others deliver below your expectations. You certainly do not want to stop your project to go to the store for a needle.

A crafts store will yield various types of needles. When possible, get a good number of assorted needles to allow a variety to test on, and choose whenever you need one. A general recommendation is to start your quilting with a fresh needle each time, but many quilters use theirs until it is blunt or broken. Whichever kind of a quilter you are, you will still need a fresh needle at some point, so having some at hand will be important.

3. Thread

There is no stitching without thread, and most projects do take up a lot of thread; you will need to be prepared. You may need a particular thread for each project, but cotton tends to be all-purpose. You can opt to stock up on a variety, depending on the kind of quilts you intend to make, or buy for each project. Thread also tends to run out very fast during stitching. You can also get assorted threads to keep at hand. Whatever you do, ensure that your choice of thread is high-quality; you do not want it to break easily. Besides, thread is what gives quilting its beauty, so do not allow your efforts to be lost because of the thread.

4. Pins

Quilting involves joining three or more layers together, and for that, you need pins to hold the fort before you can do the actual stitching. You can use any kind of pins, but those with a large head will be ideal for ease of removal. For the basting process, it is best to use safety pins to avoid pricking when handling the sandwich. Get a good number of pins that allows you to baste more than one sandwich at a time. Do not forget to get a storage container to store them safely and avoid losing them.

5. Iron

When basting, it is best to iron your fabric before spreading it on the surface. An iron board is an essential item for any quilter. Ironing your fabric ensures you don't have wrinkles, which can ruin your quilt. Ironed fabric tends to come together easily and firmly, eliminating much shifting and easing the basting and stitching processes. With the iron, it is best to also get an ironing board or suitable ironing surface to do the job. You don't need anything fancy; your regular home iron and ironing board can do the job effectively.

Above are some of the most important items you need, other than the machine and fabric. Another item you should consider is a seam ripper because, although everyone makes mistakes and undoing seams is part of quilting, as a beginner, you will make *many* mistakes. Having a seam ripper at hand will quicken the process of undoing any poorly done seams, so you can get back to stitching. Other items include a tape measure to ensure your measurements are correct and a marking tool to help mark the designs.

Quilting Tips

Quilting is a learning process that calls for commitment. As a beginner, it can be easy to feel overwhelmed by what you don't know and the high expectations. Here are a few pointers to always keep in mind before starting any project.

1. Clean Your Machine

Your machine is your main tool in free-motion quilting, and you need to take care of it. One way of doing so is to clean it by de-fluffing the bobbin case and removing the throat plate. Ensure it is clean, then oil it. Ideally, you should clean and de-lint the machine after every project or every eight to ten hours of quilting. The machine will thank you by running well, and your stitches will look good without much trouble. Of course, it is necessary to get a good quality machine from a brand that lasts.

2. Threading

First of all, you should always use quality thread; it will not break easily, nor will it leave much lint on your machine. That said, many quilters struggle with threading. An easy way to thread is to use a small amount of hair spray on the thread before rolling it between your fingers and allowing it to dry for a few seconds. The hairspray will stiffen the thread, and with a snip of the edge, you can easily poke it through the machine and needle. Alternatively, you can put a white piece of paper behind the needle to improve the visibility of its eye. If that does not appeal to you, cut your thread at a 45-degree angle to make it easy to thread.

You should ensure your spool holder is oriented correctly, so the thread can run smoothly. In most cases, the machine will come with two spool holders— a vertical and a horizontal one. The easiest way to know is by checking how the thread is wound up. Threads that are straight should go on the vertical spool holder, whereas those that form an X are best placed on the horizontal one.

3. Needle

Always use the appropriate needle, as per your project and thread. Using the wrong needle can result in breakage or frustration from inefficient quilting. Sometimes, you may need to change your needle. In that case, it is best to place it back in the container but place it the opposite way from the new needles. You can place it with the point upwards, indicating to you which one is the used needle. Also, if your machine starts to skip stitches, it is time to change your needle and clean up the bobbin case.

4. Fabric Cutting

Invest in a good, solid pair of scissors, and don't lose it—it will be one of your most important assets. Keep it for its chosen purpose and do not yield to the temptation to snip on a piece of paper with them. If you can, get a different pair of scissors for silk.

You should always measure twice to be certain. Remember that cutting cannot be undone. Also, ensure that you add an extra inch to the edge of the quilt; that way, you can easily stitch close to where the binding will be done.

If you are struggling with making your fabric taut but not stretch and achieving a wrinkle-free finish, try spray basting. For the smoothness in the curves, a key tip is to use many pins, each taking only a small bite of the fabric.

5. Stitching

Remember that in free-motion stitching, you are the one in control. Find a good room to quilt in with adequate lighting and make it your happy place.

You may struggle to quilt lines with a good level of accuracy. When possible, I hold my ruler with both hands for added stability. I can easily go around a curve while holding the ruler in both hands. I like to have some of my fingers on the ruler and some on the fabric, since it helps give me a sense of grounding. However, there is still a high chance that the stitches will be uneven. Aim for consistency, and you will see tangible results.

No matter how bad you think the quilt is, finish it. There is a sense of satisfaction in finishing a project, even if it looks imperfect. Embrace those ugly stitches—they are how you work to get more even and beautiful stitches.

Chapter Summary

Your first stitches will always remain some of the most memorable ones, mostly because they are also likely to be some of the most ugly ones. Remember that:

- Whatever you do, make sure you quilt; you can only get better.

- Always take on small projects first and finish them.

- Quilting is an experience; learn through the stitches.

- Always secure your first stitches by double stitching them so they do not run.

- Be kind to yourself and enjoy the process.

In the next chapter, you will learn about tension, which is one of the most important things that affect the quilting journey. Tension can make or break your thread, so you will need to know when and how to adjust it.

Chapter Eight: Tension

Finding the right tension is crucial for creating beautiful stitches during free-motion quilting. On the flip side, get it wrong, and you end up with ugly stitches and loops. Your confidence level when it comes to tension may be low, but this is free-motion quilting. Here, anything is possible. Besides, you have this guide to help you through the process.

Needle-Thread Tension

Let us address the top tension first. If you remember, during threading, we talked about putting your thread through discs and ensuring it is secured properly. Top tension refers to the tension that emanates from the discs found at the front of your machine, which in turn affects the needle thread. In an ideal tension situation, there is a neutral tug of war between the top and bottom stitch, with the twist of the thread falling in the middle of the batting.

Tension Troubleshooting Tips

As with anything else, preparation is key. You do not want to spend hours adjusting tension without success simply because you and your machine are not ready. Hence, it is important to ensure that you:

- Have a needle that is oriented correctly to your machine; a fresh one would be ideal.

- Check that there is no lint in your machine. Lint could contribute to tension issues.

- Do not forget the presser foot. You will need to raise it when adjusting tension, but lower it when it is time to sew.

- Coordinate the needle size correctly to the thread size. For example, you can pair a thread of 40 weight with a needle of size 90/14.

- Use good quality thread; check for age and quality.

- Check the way the thread winds onto the bobbin. If it is wound in a crisscross, you may need to lift it off the spool and string through the machine.

- Thread your bobbin correctly; that is, evenly and with good pressure.

Adjusting Tension

To adjust tension, you need to raise the presser foot, and on a digital machine, select either a higher or lower number, depending on whether you want it tight or loose. If you are using an analog machine and lack the option to select numbers, all you have to do is turn the knob to either tighten or loosen it. You would then lower the presser foot, stitch, and check to see if everything is working as it should. Always remember that a high number means a higher tension, whereas a smaller number means reduced tension. When adjusting the tension, it is best to reduce or increase by half a number and test it out until it is right. Here is a more elaborate method of adjusting tension.

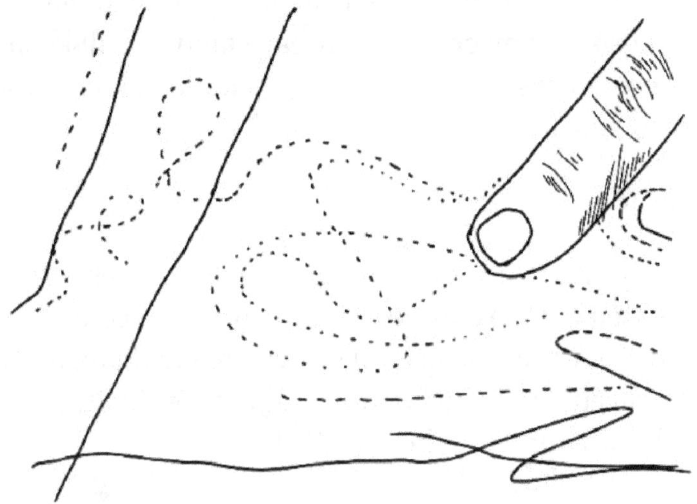

Thread Needle Thread (TNT) Method

Thread

Completely re-thread your machine from the spool. You can refer to your machine's manual for specifics on threading or online if you don't have the manual. You should make sure your threading is done as recommended by the manufacturer to avoid any errors. Once done, do a few stitches and check for the quality. If not, move to the needle.

An important point to note is that you cannot have proper tension without threading your machine correctly. The tension discs, thread guides, tension regulator, and bobbin-case spring all work together to ensure simultaneous flow of tread from the bobbin and the needle, allowing for the production of a symmetrical stitch.

To avoid any further tension issues due to the thread spool, you can use a thread stand. It will keep the tension even by creating a constant tension on the thread spool.

Needle

Now it's time to change the needle. Earlier, we discussed how to choose the appropriate needle. Choose one and replace what was already there. A top stitch needle is a good option, but ensure that the needle size matches the thread size.

Tension

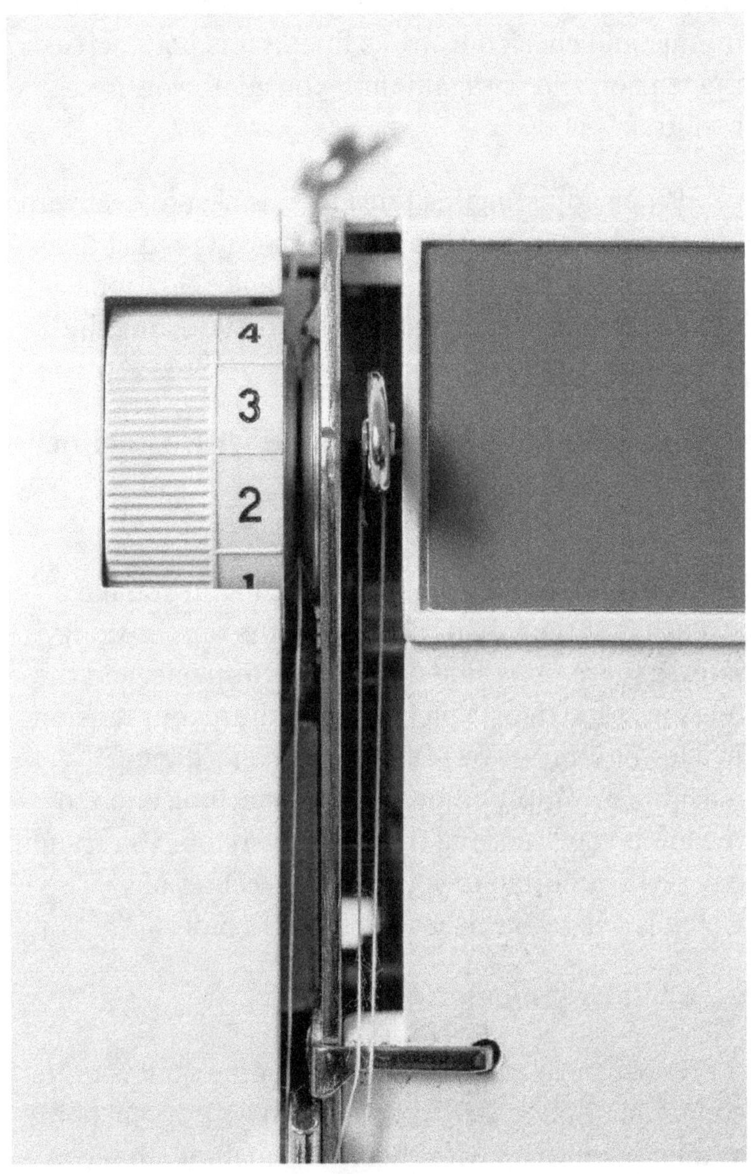

Always start by turning your machine's tension controls to zero and practice with a similar sandwich to the actual project to see if the tension is alright. Have the darning foot on and stitch for about half a minute and check if it works fine. If it is not, increase the tension and try again until you get the desired results.

When adjusting the tension, it is best to deal with one variable at a time; that way you can predict the outcome and move to the next variable. Let's look at some common problems that call for adjusting the tension.

Common Problems Associated with Tension

1. Top Eyelashes

Eyelashes refer to extreme looping. If you have eyelashes at the top, it means that the top thread is pulling more to its side than the bottom one, and the tension is too tight. You can then adjust your tension to a lower number by selecting one on a digital machine or simply adjusting your machine knob to the left if you are using the analog version. You should pay extra attention to your stitches' center of swirls, which is where eyelashes are likely to hide.

2. Back Eyelashes

Having eyelashes on the back of the quilt is quite common. Chances are high that you will, at one point or another, end up with them. The inability to see at the back as you quilt is a major contributing factor. Quilters usually realize that the back has eyelashes *way* after doing a considerable amount of work. Sometimes, it is only as you take a well-deserved break and admire your work that you start to notice. If you end up with eyelashes on the back, it simply means that the tension at the top is too loose.

The solution is to tighten or increase your top tension by putting your machine on a higher number or adjusting your knob correctly if using an analog machine.

3. Floaters

Sometimes, the stitches can opt to float away. Instead of creating an eyelash, the thread may appear to be "floating" on the quilt's back, though you can, in some instances, feel some bumps, despite the top thread barely showing. You can eliminate such a problem by increasing the top tension to ensure nice stitches both at the back and on top of the quilt.

4. Broken Thread

Broken thread is also a common occurrence, even more than having eyelashes on top of the quilt. In most cases, it is as a result of the top tension being too tight, and a quick adjustment should resolve it. However, if that does not sort out the issue, look at other factors like the presence of a burr on your needle plate or foot and checking that the presser foot is not too high.

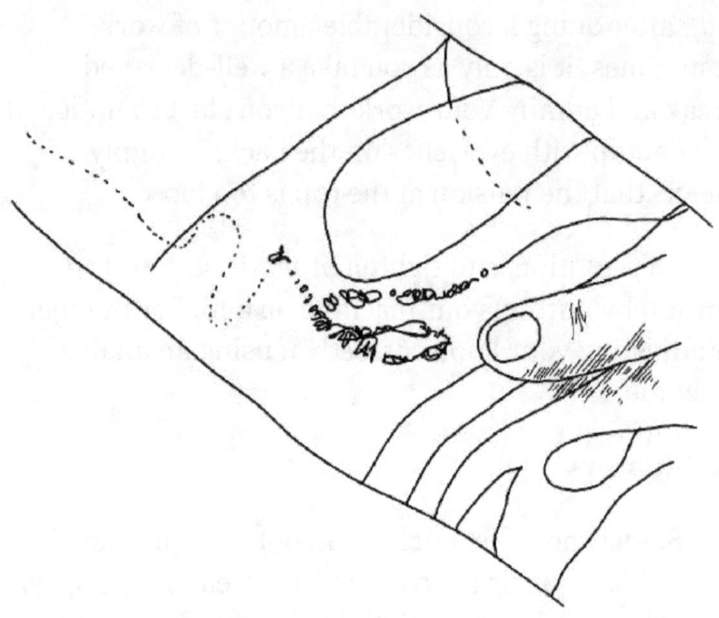

Having your tension too loose or too tight can make the rest of your work quite time-consuming. Although you may adjust your tension, the eyelashes and floaters are still on the quilt and call for unpicking. It is annoying and frustrating, but that is the only way to correct the stitches. To avoid such a situation, it is best to always check your tension.

When to Do the Tension Check

- **Before Any New Project**—After setting up your machine, adjust the tension and quilt a few stitches to make sure the tension is right.

- **Whenever You Go Back to Quilting**—If you leave your project lying around for some time—and it happens often—especially with all other responsibilities waiting, remember to check the tension.

- At the Start of a Thread Color, Bobbin, or Inserting a New Needle—Always ensure the new thread and needle are well-adjusted.

You may think that checking the tension will take much time and reduce your quilting time. Well, it will take a few moments and save you hours and frustration of unpicking down the road. Besides, the aim of quilting is to create a beautiful masterpiece, and tension plays a major role in that.

During tension testing, it is best to stitch some zigzags and loops because tension issues mainly show up at points and curves.

If you cannot clear your tension problems and can still see those little dots forming on either side of the quilt, still don't let that stop you from quilting. You can still use a camouflage quilt back, as there are occasionally problems that cannot be solved.

Chapter Summary

Getting the tension right is an important part of free-motion quilting.

- Remember to check for the correct tension before starting a stitch.

- Use the Thread-Needle-Tension method to get it just right.

- The thread and needle influence tension, but so do other factors, including the environment.

- You can start from zero tension and keep adjusting until you get the right stitches.

In the next chapter, you will actually get started. We will look at doodling and getting your project off the ground.

Chapter Nine:
Getting Started

Free-motion quilters have a saying that, "What is the top always stays at the top." In essence, this means that you do not need to do much flipping fabrics or twisting and turning. You only need to move your fabric as a whole in your direction of choice.

Let's look at how to free-motion quilt in a few steps.

Free-Motion Quilting Made Easy

1. **Prepare a Fabric Sandwich for Practice**—Since you have a good understanding of how to baste, you may enjoy the practice by making another sandwich—which could be relatively smaller—for you to test on. You have to test everything before actually quilting, lest it cost you hours and frustrate you.

   The practice sandwich should ideally be made from the same fabric as your project. It's not a waste of any new fabric; it is so that you can get the same feel and results as the main project.

   For example, if your project is made of cotton, and your practice sandwich is made of silk, the suitable thread and needle will differ. What will work on the sandwich may be horrendous on the actual project. To avoid that, make two sets of sandwiches using the same materials, one for the project and the other for the practice sandwich.

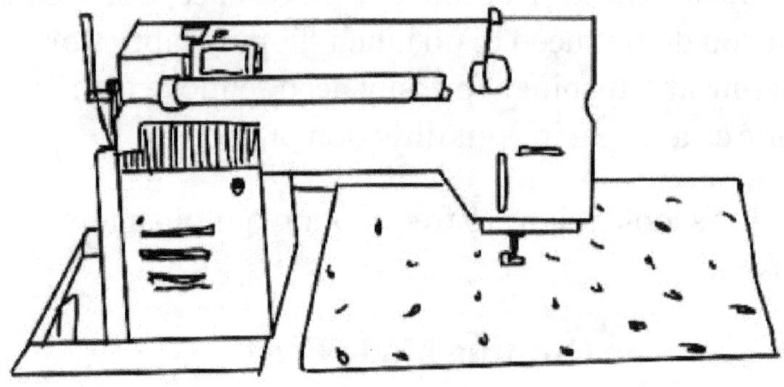

2. **Start Doodling**—Although you can find many patterns online, it is best to doodle yourself as you see fit. Like free-motion quilting, doodling does not come with a book of rules. You can move your quilt in any direction, which helps you set your wand. You can either let go and doodle freehand or make a particular pattern.

    You can opt to start doodling from a piece of paper to gain confidence before shifting that to your practice sandwich. Some quilters develop a habit of doodling in a book during their free time to perfect their hand and come up with interesting patterns.

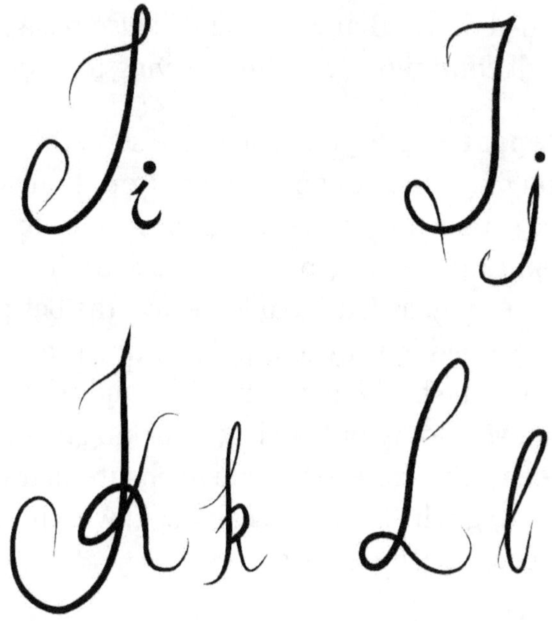

3. **Start with Doodling a Cursive L**—One of the simplest letters of the alphabet to write is L. Make fun of it by turning it into an entire pattern. There are many interesting ways to write the letter L, and your imagination is your only limit. Did you know you can even draw a bird out of a simple L? Everything is possible with doodling. You can also do the cursive C, which will prepare you for feather designs. Other letters of the alphabet can become some of the best patterns. Get your pen or pencil out and start doodling.

For free-motion quilting, it is best to use continuous lines. Draw without putting the pencil down; that way, you will also be able to quilt continuously without having to stop.

4. **Repeat**—Once you have made something that you like—an L, or any other pattern that you are satisfied with—repeat it until you can replicate the same pattern. You see why you need a paper? The goal is to have the pattern embedded in your brain. Most times, after a while, the brain may play tricks and tell you that you got it, only to begin making mistakes. Keep going for a long time to ensure that you *really* got it. Then, you can begin working on your practice sandwich.

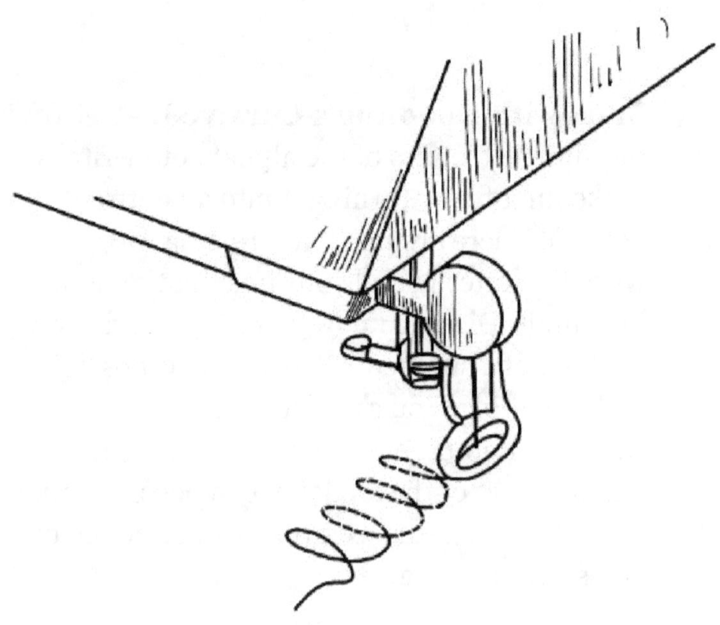

5. **Maintain a Certain Speed**—Once you have your doodle well-settled in a good space in your brain, it is time for speed. You want to maintain a particular speed to keep your stitches even when quilting. Practice makes perfect. Keep practicing, but with a focus on doodling at a certain speed for each doodle.

6. **Match Your Movement Speed to Your Machine Speed**—How fast you move your fabric also depends on the speed of your machine. You need to strike a balance between the two; otherwise, moving one faster than the other can result in eyelashes and ugly looping. Remember that pushing hard on the machine will increase the speed considerably. Also, do not hurry over the top when doing sharp or curved designs, as it can result in a longer stitch length that could ruin your pattern. Keep playing with it, pushing on the foot pedal and moving your hands. The goal is not to do it too fast; this is not a race. What you are aiming for is consistency.

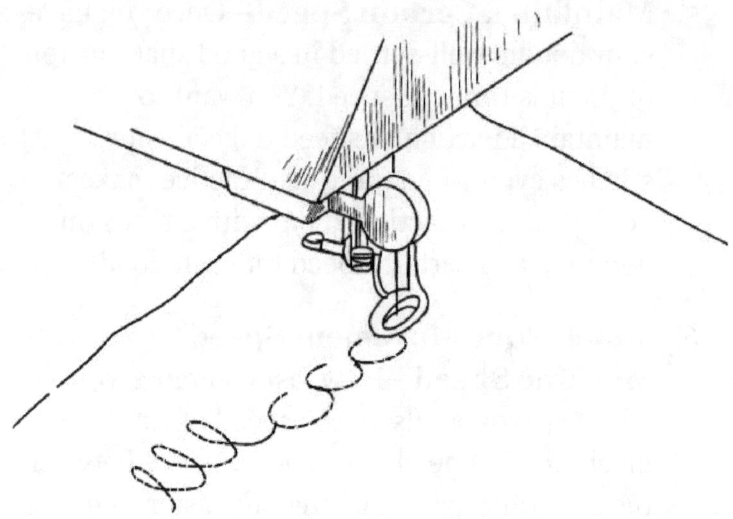

7. **Experiment with Threads**—Once you have a good rhythm and can move your sandwich in time with the machine, you need to choose the best combination of needle and thread. Needle and thread are important in making the perfect stitch. You need to ensure that the needle is fit for the fabric and will not cause damage. The thread also has to work well with the needle and bring out the beauty of the quilt. The good news is that you have a chance to try out as many needle-thread combinations as you wish, until you find exactly what you are looking for. Remember to write down the combinations as you try them on your practice sandwich.

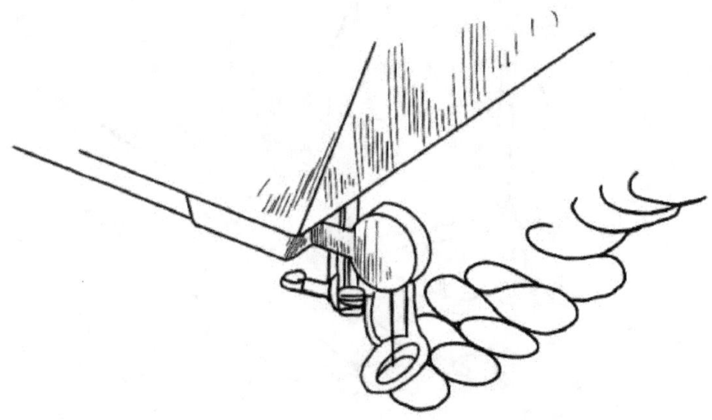

8. **Quilt**—When you find the right doodle and
   have the perfect needle and thread, it is time to
   quilt, though still on your practice sandwich.
   You should keep quilting the pattern, balancing
   the speed, and practicing until you get even
   stitches. However, do not be afraid to try out a
   real project once you think you're ready. In a
   short while, you will look back at your first
   quilt with pride at how far you have come.

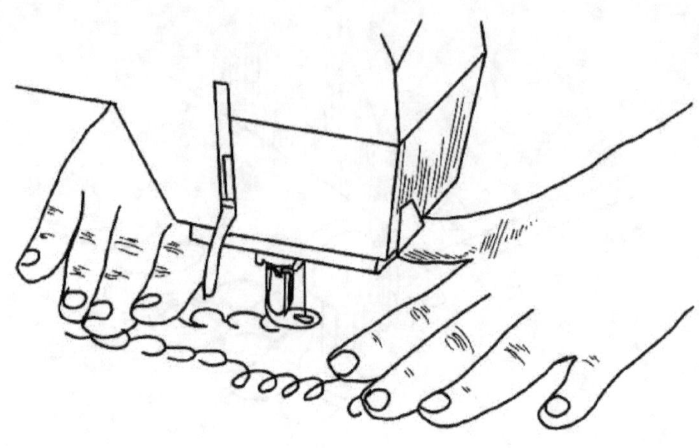

Practice

The only way to get perfect stitches and make beautiful, error-free patterns is through practice. You should make several practice sandwiches of different fabric and use them to figure out which ones work well with different patterns and threads. Do not tire from trying out different designs on your practice sandwiches; at the end of the day, you will be proud of the project you undertake. You will have an opportunity to create doodles that are unique to you, know your preferred needles, and understand which fabric pairs best with which thread.

Chapter Summary

The only sure way to get started is by doing and doodling. Do so, and you're on your way to becoming an expert free-motion quilter.

- Doodle away! You can start with cursive letters.

- Draw on paper before moving to stitching.

- Practice your name; charity begins at home.

- Mistakes are the pathways to greatness and perfection, so embrace them.

In the next chapter, you will have an opportunity to create and stitch your first design!

Chapter Ten: Making Your First Design

Since you have been practicing your doodling and have a solid grasp on your foot-hand coordination, it is time to create your first design. Yes, you are now transitioning from a beginner to a quilter with a little experience. In this chapter, you will get the opportunity and guidance to create your first quilt design. We will start simple and easy to get your confidence levels up. As usual, here is a step-by-step guide on creating your first design.

What You Need:

1. Threads

2. Needle according to thread

3. Quilt

Steps:

1. **Create Your Quilt Sandwich**—You may not be very enthusiastic about the taping down of the fabric and putting all those pins, but stay encouraged. This particular sandwich is for your first design. You can start with a small quilt sandwich that will not take a long time to baste. As you begin, working on smaller projects is helpful because they will be easier to

complete. Also, in case of mistakes, it is also faster to undo stitches from a small quilt than a large one. Once you are confident of your ability to design and quilt, you can gradually increase the size of your project.

2. **Prepare Your Machine**—Clean and oil your machine, prepare it as we discussed, and put in a new needle and thread, ready to quilt.

3. **Position Your Quilt**—You need your quilt to be right under the needle point where you want to start. Ideally, it is recommended to start quilting in the middle and move around to keep the sandwich from shifting. However, this is free-motion quilting, meaning you can begin from anywhere. The key determinant of where to start lies in your design and intended pattern.

4. **Start Quilting**—Lower the presser foot and begin quilting. How hard you drive the presser foot determines how fast your machine moves. You can either go slowly or fast—the choice is yours.

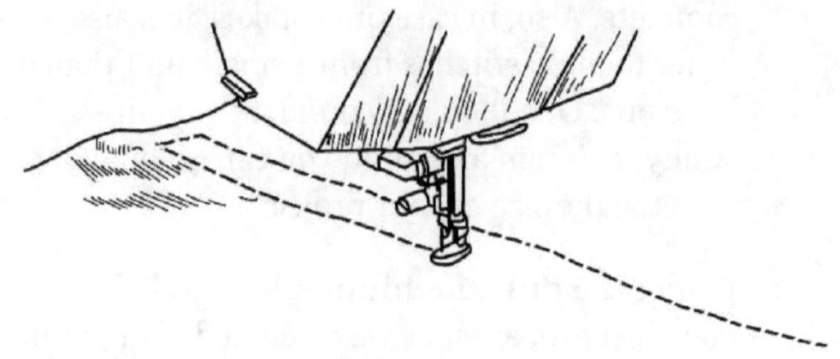

5. **Move the Quilt**—In free-motion quilting, you have to remember that you are in control. Move the quilt at a constant pace. You need to find a balanced rhythm between your hands and feet to avoid looping. You are now creating stitches on your quilt. These stitches put together make your design.

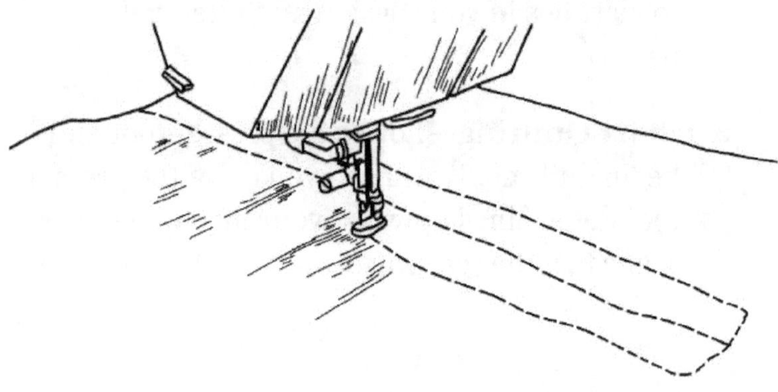

Let us look at some designs.

Simple Beginner Designs

a) Straight Lines

Some of the easiest stitches to do include making straight lines. If you are unsure of making your line straight, take a ruler and draw the line with a suitable marker. You can stitch along the line. Do not be overly concerned that your stitches are not even; your hand is the guide, and like everything human, there is no perfection. Strive for consistency while moving the quilt sandwich and keep in mind how hard you are pushing on the presser foot.

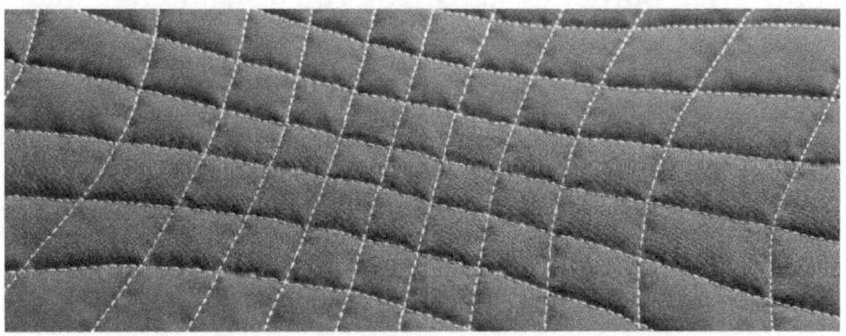

You can have straight lines on your borders or have them spit your quilt into two. You could have a series of straight or crisscrossing lines. Whatever you choose to do, it's all up to you, just keep your eye on the line and quilt away. There is always an element of elegance in simplicity. You may be amazed at the results.

b) Cursive Letters

In the previous chapter, we practiced cursive letters, and now is the time to apply them. The cursive L and C are particularly easy to apply and can be part of your designs. The cursive C may call for backing up on your line of stitching. Many beginners are scared of doing so, but you should not worry; there is nothing wrong with backing up on your stitches if you have to.

Cursive Es are also an easy beginner design to practice. You make them either straight up or upside down. From these, you can create loops, figure 8s, and some great border designs. You can also stitch them close together, meandering across the quilt to create a flowery pattern. Really, there is no limit to what simple cursive Es can achieve.

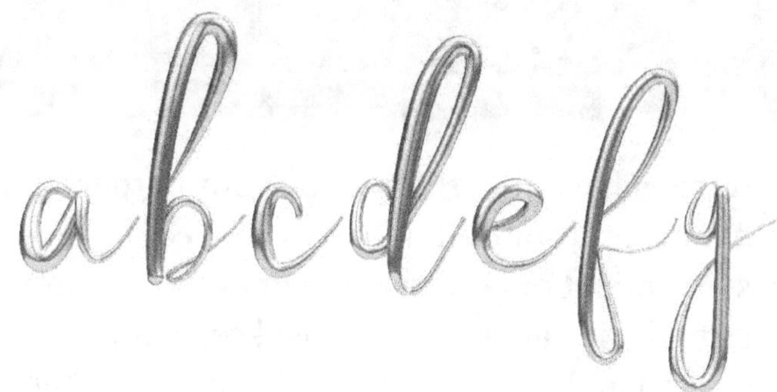

You can try writing your name on the quilt and even opt for your initials. Try quilting some letters on your sandwich. Free-motion quilting calls for using your imagination, do not limit yourself. Again, there is no hurry in free-motion stitching. Take as much as you need to get it right.

c) Loop da Loop

Meandering around the quilt is a good way to have fun and let your imagination run wild while still creating a beautiful design. Loops can also emulate cursive writing and are a good place to begin. Additionally, loops are great for filling an open background and just quilting around. Once you make a loop, you can stop where the threads cross and move to the opposite direction for the next loop. Having your loops opposite each other yet interconnected is a great way to create a random feel across the quilt. You can have big loops or small loops, or even mix them. Do what you please, as long as you are quilting.

As with all other designs, you can opt to draw them on the fabric to improve your confidence. Don't worry if you don't always land on the lines; they are there for general guidance and will wash off, leaving your stitches. Focus more on maintaining the speed of your hand in turn with that of your machine.

d) Flowers

You are probably thinking flowers are tough, and you're getting nervous. Relax—if you can loop, you can make a flower. Think of a simple flower; it is made of loops and a small circle in the middle. Now you can loop, which means you can conquer the flower. Make a loop for a petal and add a circle in the middle. The circle gives you a reference point of where to end your loop. Loop around, always going back to the circle, and you have a flower!

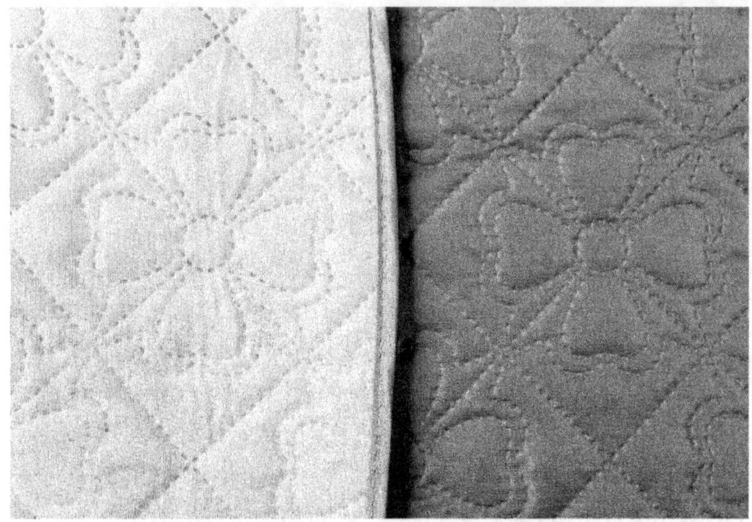

You can use a guide grip to help you make the loops and scallops, which are part of your flower. Meander around, leaving a flower here and there, and soon, you will have a beautiful design.

e) Pebbles

Pebbles are merely circles and a classic filler design. Besides being simple to make, you can use them in different ways either by piling them together or scattering them across the quilt. However you chose to position your pebbles, they are a great design to incorporate. A tip to making the circles even, clean, and smooth is to look ahead. Your hands instinctively move toward your gaze. Look ahead, and your pebbles will be smooth. The size of the pebbles will depend entirely on you.

f) Switchbacks

You see that space between parallel lines? An ideal design for it is switchbacks. Switchbacks include designs that call for a back and forth movement, such as Us and Ns. They are also ideal for borders or sashing.

The key to making beautiful back and forths is to keep the lines about the same height, parallel, and straight as well as you can, with the curves nice and round. If need be, you can mark your quilt to help you trace the back and forth movement better.

g) Figure 8

Much like writing the eight, this design calls for stitching loops that resemble the number eight. Similar to switchbacks, you need to keep the top and bottom curved areas nice and round and relatively the same size.

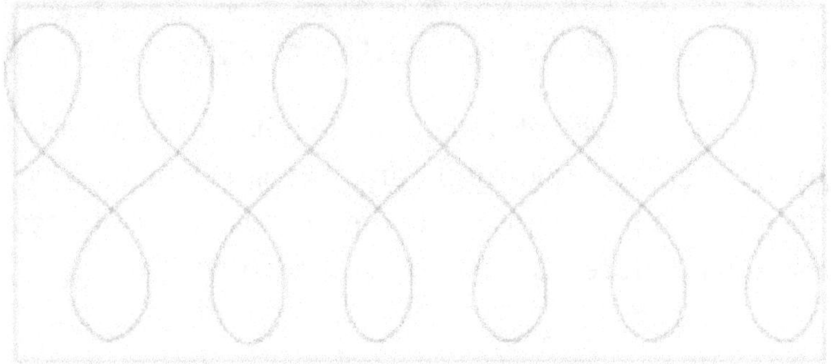

h) Spirals

As the name suggests, this design involves making spiral lines on your quilt. The good news is that you can add your own flair. You can have rounded or pointed ones, depending on your preference and texture. You can also change the spacing between the lines. The most important thing to remember when stitching spirals is to allow yourself space to leave the inside of the spiral.

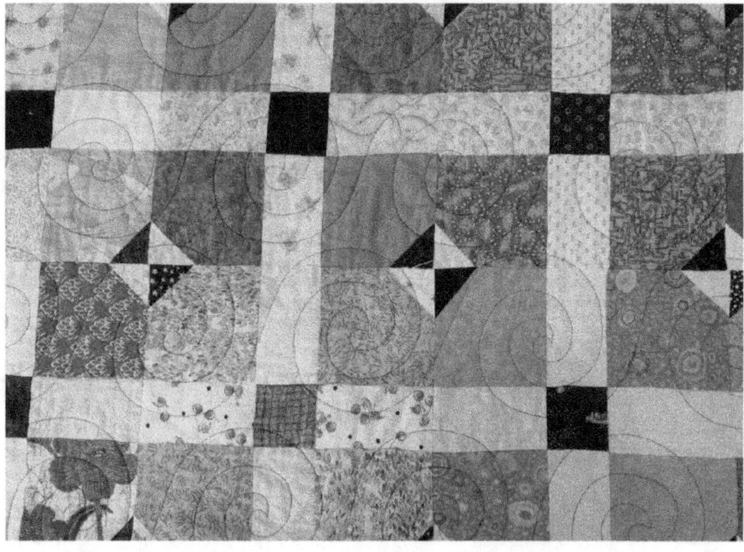

An advantage of this method is that it allows you to travel all over your quilt, and you can even echo the design. You may want to doodle the design first to get used to it before starting up your machine.

i) Star

You can also create a star design by moving the quilt in a star shape. You may want to pause slightly at the top to give your mind a chance to readjust in that direction and prevent it from making more of a curve than a sharp tip.

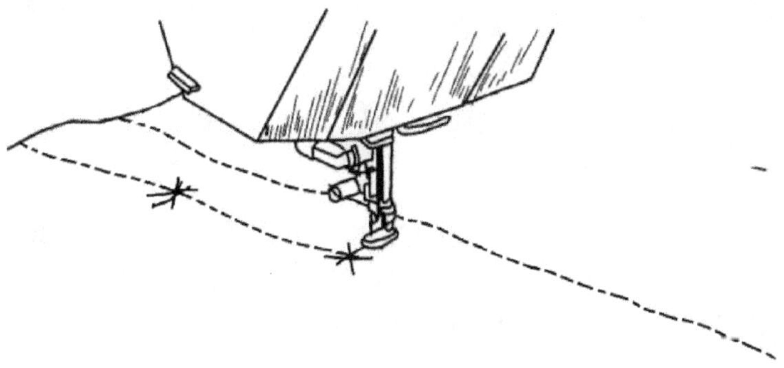

j) Stippling

Stippling is probably the most quilted design in the history of quilting, and for a good reason; it goes anywhere and adds texture very quickly. For ease of understanding, stippling is merely wiggly lines or meandering without ever crossing stitches. You can make your stitches sharp or round, depending on your preference. Yours may look different from the others.

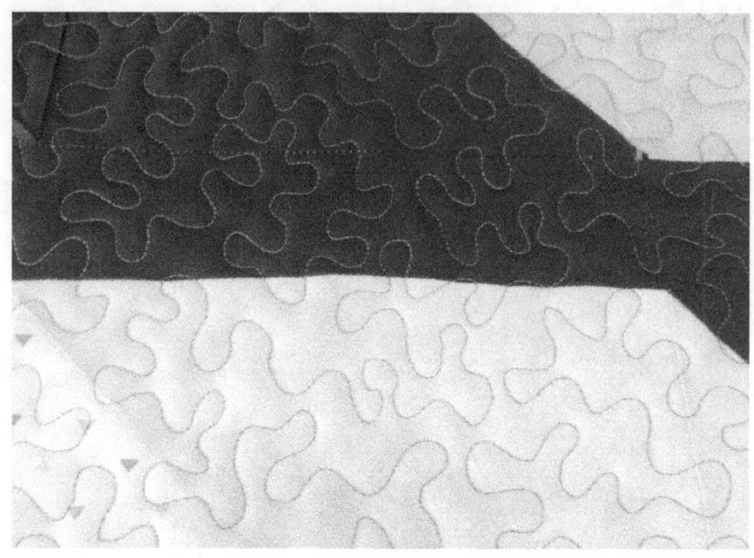

What you need to keep in mind is how to get out of tight areas and keep quilting. If you get to the edge, you can tie off your stitching and move on to another spot.

k) Pumpkins

Pumpkins are quite pretty, and they look just as beautiful on quilts. As a beginner, you can learn how to quilt pumpkins. They do not have to be perfect—after all, they come in all sizes and shapes. Once you have mastered the loop, you can do the pumpkin. The best way is to start from the top, traveling around to make the external shell, dropping down the middle and up again, before making a sort-of rectangle stem at the top. You can then get out by making vines, either via single loops or meanders to the next pumpkin. You need to keep in mind where to get out of your pumpkin and make the next one.

Consider drawing the design on a piece of paper and practicing, so you can have a good feel of it before you begin stitching.

l) Paisley

When creating a paisley design on your quilt, you would start with a teardrop shape and pivot and echo around the teardrop. As you echo, increase the distance between the curves, but decrease the distance as you go back to the starting point. This is the basic design. From there you can echo the teardrop as much as you want and branch out to start another teardrop, angling in a different direction. Repeat the process.

The examples given here are only a guide to get you started. However, there is no limit to what design you can choose for your quilt. Below is a suggestion of a quilting design for you to start with.

Sample Design

You can begin by combing a straight line and a star. From the left corner, stitch a straight line and set a particular distance to create a star by quickly moving the quilt into a star shape. The distance between stars will depend on the length of your quilt and your preference. You can repeat the pattern by stitching in uneven rows. Creating uneven rows helps disguise the rows of stitching on the quilt. The key here is to work systematically from one row to the next.

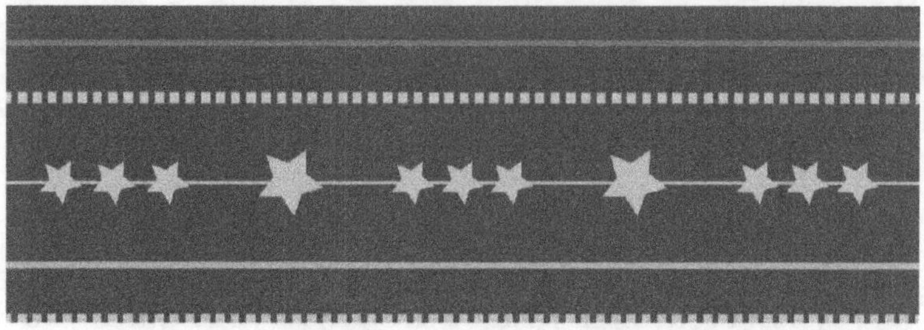

In the middle of the quilt, you can free-handedly write your name or any other text of your choice before proceeding with the line and star design. If you are nervous, you can mark the pattern and trace your name on the fabric. That way, you can have something to follow as a guide.

In no time, you will have created your very first design. Congratulations! You are on your way to becoming a celebrated quilter.

Chapter Summary

Developing and executing a design of your own is not rocket science. All the designs you see on quilts are products of people like you. Remember:

- There is no limit to what you can create.

- Start with simple designs; even straight lines, can make a beautiful design.

- Gradually take on more designs in scope and details.

- Always draw your design on paper to give your mind a chance to internalize it before transferring it to the quilt.

- Practice.

In the next chapter, we look at filler designs and how to use them to make your quilt more or less engaging.

Chapter Eleven: Filler Designs

Choosing a Filler Design

Although it may seem easy, choosing a good filler design can turn into a tricky affair. You could choose a filler that will not blend well with your choice of a design and make your quilt look different from what you intended. In most cases, your choice of a filler design will be largely dependent on the kind of texture you want in your quilt. For example, you may choose to have a lot of movement in one particular area and none in another. You could also choose to have an even texture across the entire project.

The trick to selecting a great filler design for your quilt lies in the amount of contrast you prefer. If you want to showcase your main design and make it pop, then you will need a contrasting filler. On the other hand, you can choose a blending filler to hide the main design or make it subtle. Filler designs can also hide your imperfections, thus making your quilt a masterpiece, regardless of any mistakes. Keep in mind that the level of contrast is determined by the design shape, thread color, design direction, and filler's density.

Creating your Filler Design

You now know what a filler is and can now choose which type to use in which situation. You probably have a preference already. Now is the time to create a filler design of your own.

What You Need

1. Threads.

2. Fabric.

3. Needle according to thread.

Steps

1. **Prepare Your Quilt Sandwich**—Choose what kind of quilt you want to create and go through the basting process. Even for smaller projects, you will have to ensure that your sandwich is done properly. Remember to keep it taut but not stretched. The choice of how big a quilt you should make is solely yours. As a suggestion, beginners should use a smaller quilt, just to see a finished product and keep them encouraged. Even going through the basting process for a small project will give you experience and help you improve.

2. **Prepare Your Machine**—If you have been using the machine, clean it to get rid of any lint, then oil it. You want your machine running smoothly and without much inhibitions. Put

your thread and needle in and ensure you opt for the needle down setting. That way, you can move your fabric in the direction you want while it is well-anchored by the needle.

3. **Position the Sandwich Under the Needle**—You want your starting point to be sitting right on the needle, so when you press down on the presser foot, all you would have to do is move the fabric and get quilting. It is recommendable that you have a general idea of your design, so you can know where to start from and in which direction to follow.

4. **Quilt a Boundary**—You need to quilt the boundary so you can have a marked beginning and end to work with. You can do simple double lines and make a pattern in between the lines, like pebbles or even swirls.

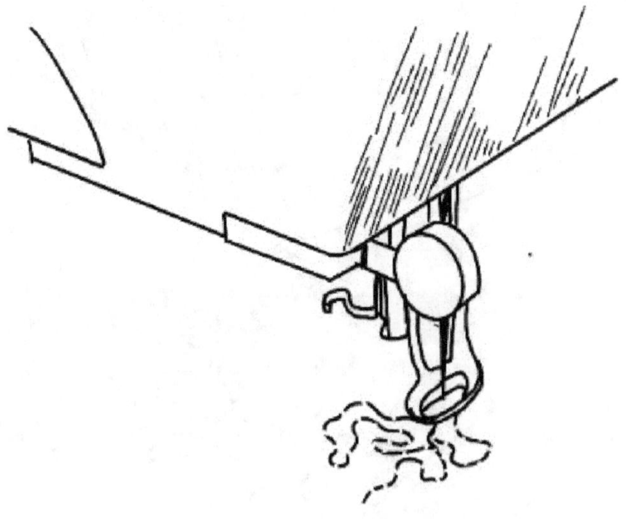

5. **Quilt Your Design Freehand**—With clearly marked boundaries, it is now time to quilt. You can quilt your design of choice freehand.

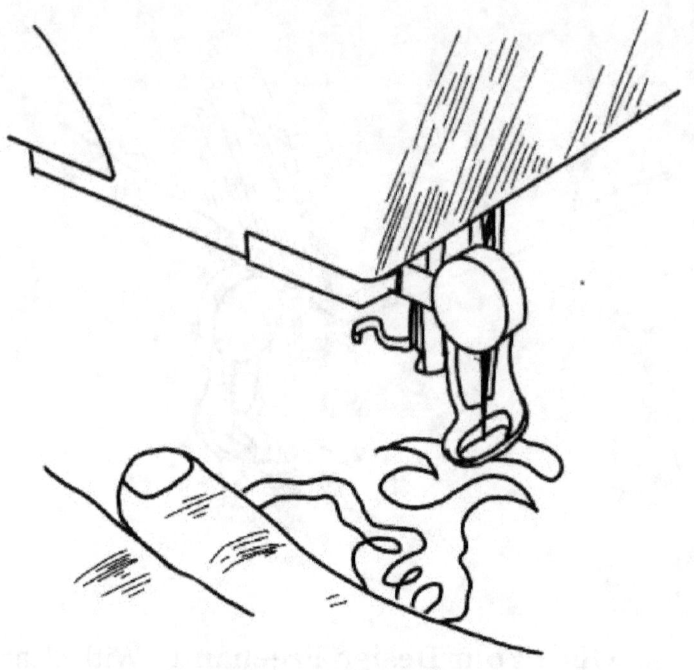

6. **Use Fillers**—Most often, there will only be so much of the design you can quilt. For example, if you choose to quilt huts, you will have spaces between them. That is where the fillers come in. As another example, you could stitch a name at the center of the quilt, though such a design leaves the quilt looking empty. Filler designs are meant to fill the open parts of the quilt and draw attention to the central design. Meanders, pebbles, stipples, snowflakes, and loops are all great fillers. Once you have the hang of them, you can stitch all over the quilt without any problems.

You can make smaller versions of your central designs be fillers. For example, if you are stitching spiralling circles, you can make small pebbles or spirals across the quilt.

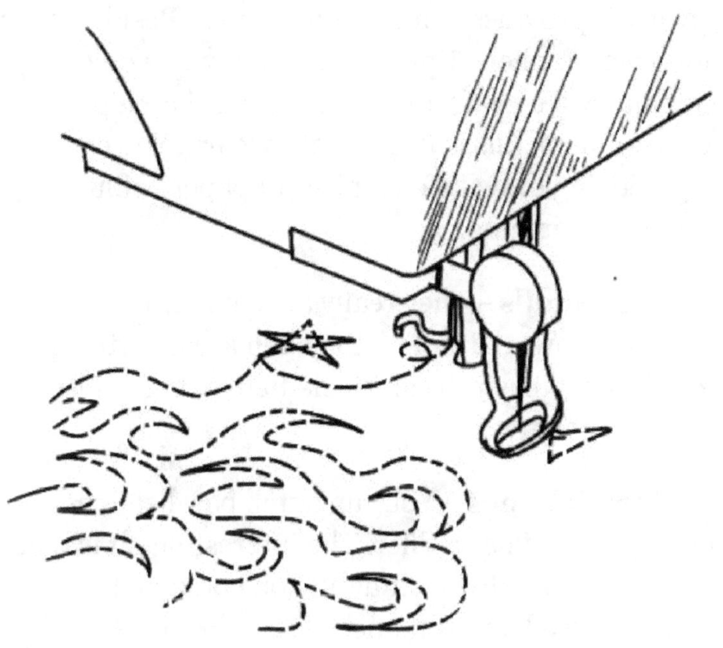

7. **Secure Your Design**—You certainly do not want to have your stitches running, not after all the hard work you put in. Therefore, you need to secure your stitches as you start and end. Simply make two stitches and go back on them to ensure they do not run. In most cases, the repetition will be hardly visible.

Some Common Filler Designs

Stippling—As the ultimate quilting design, stippling has been and continues to be one of the most used filler designs. We all love stippling so much because it provides texture and interest. Besides, as an independent filler, stippling goes anywhere on the quilt and can even form the background for a pattern. For beginners, this is important to learn. You can start by practicing drawing on a piece of paper before moving to stitching.

Clamshells—They really are semi-circles stacked in rows that fill up the open areas on the quilt beautifully. Since you can stack them, you can also use them in tight areas.

Parallel lines—You can stitch parallel lines across your quilt as a filler. The interesting bit is that they do not have to be straight; you could make them wavy or curved, or even uneven.

Pebbles—Pebbles add texture and draw interest in a quilt. You would start by stitching a simple circle, then add another next to it. Keep adding until you cover the space you need. You can vary the size.

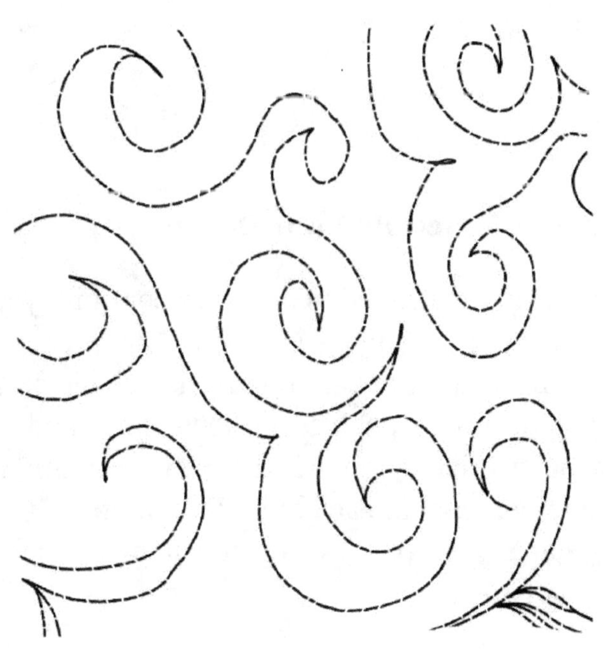

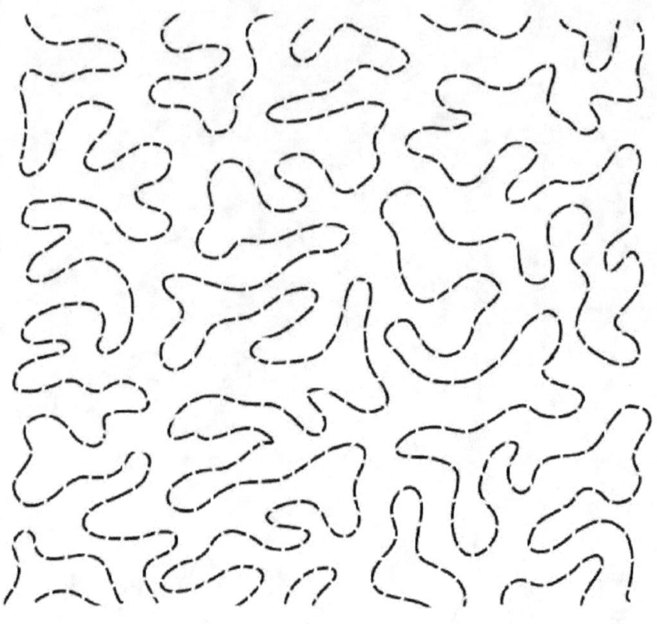

Mixing and Matching Your Design

You are not restricted to one filler per quilt; you can have as many as you please and either spread them across the quilt or vary them per each block. You can use, for example, pebbles, nested spirals, and lines to make a rich texture. Create your own unique design and personalize each quilt. Free-motion quilting starts with "free," so feel free to make each quilt your own.

Chapter Summary

Filler designs can either make your main design to pop or take attention away from it. From the chapter, we learned that:

- There are many types of filler designs, including independent stippling, pivotal, stacked, central, echo, and edge-to-edge.

- Your choice of filler will depend on your intended overall look and the spaces you are working with. Some fillers won't work for small and tight spaces.

- You are not restricted to any one filler; you can mix some together.

You are now a quilter if you have implemented what we have learned so far. All you have to do is keep practicing, and you should be a pro in no time. To keep the practice up, in the next chapter, we will make a Christmas gift. You can make as many as you want for friends and relatives.

Chapter Twelve: How to Make Sashes and Borders

Sashes

Sashes are strips of fabric that frame the quilt block, making it easy to distinguish your blocks, or make them pop. The block could be a single piece or several. Ideally, sashing is between 2½ inches to 3½ inches wide.

Here is a simple guide on how to make sashes for your quilt.

1. **Lay Out** Your **Blocks in the Preferred Order**—Take the first block and put strips on each side, then pin.

2. **Stitch**—The seam allowance should be about ¼ inch. When in doubt of where to stitch, always do ¼ inch. Make your stitches as even as possible.

3. **Press**—After stitching, take your iron box and press the opposite side first before turning your fabric, while also pressing the top part. Once you press, the seams should go out toward the sashing.

4. **Second and Subsequent Blocks**—Take the second block and stitch ¼ inch, press the

opposite side, then the top side, ensuring that the seams go toward the sashing. Repeat the process for all the blocks.

5. **The Edges**—When you get to the edge, add another piece of sashing. Remember that you will have borders to work on.

6. **Join the Rows**—Once done, measure the length of the quilt and add some inches, about 2½ inches. Stitch the sashing, then join to the subsequent row. Ensure the seam comes in towards the sashing, leaving your blocks with no bumps.

7. **Trim Off Excess**—Take a ruler and measure excess fabric to remove. Your top fabric is now ready for basting.

Borders

Your quilt isn't quite complete without borders. Borders on a quilt help bring out its center and give it a sense of wholeness. When it comes to borders, you have many options—you can have a simple strip or make them intricately pieced. Alternatively, you can simply have a straight border.

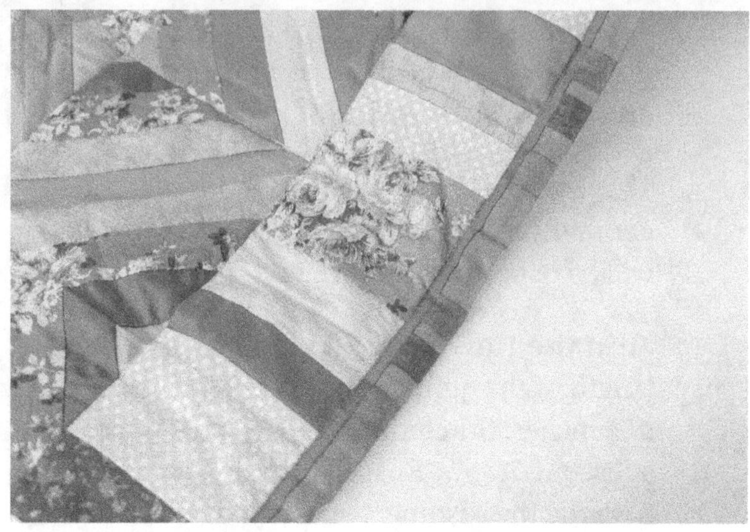

As a beginner, you may want to keep your borders simple. Here are some options:

- **Strips**—You can add strips of a single fabric around the sides of the quilt. Make border strips in pairs and add them to opposite edges.

- **Straight Borders**—In many cases, the sides of a quilt will differ in length because of stretching during quilting. To maintain a good shape and look, many quilters opt to measure the length and width of the quilt from its top to the bottom through the midpoint, so they can get the appropriate measurements. From then, it is easy to sew borders to the two longest sides before moving to the shortest sides.

Other quilters decide to measure the quilt at multiple points, then get the average of them and consider that to be the running length.

Quilting the First Two Borders

Here is a simple guide on how to sew the initial two borders on your quilt.

1. **Find the Midpoint**—You can achieve this by folding one of the borders crosswise in half to find its midpoint and crease it a little at that spot. You also need to find the horizontal midpoint of the quilt.

2. **Carefully Place the Border**—You should have your border placed along the quilt's side. Be careful to ensure that the right sides are together with matching midpoints. You can pin the border to the quilt to prevent it from shifting.

3. **Match the Bottom Border to the Bottom Edge**—As you did with the top, ensure that your bottom border matches the quilt's edge and pin them together. You may have to ensure that you pin at close intervals to ensure the lengths match well and raw edges are well-aligned on the entire side of the quilt.

4. **Sew the Borders**—You can use a seam allowance of ¼ inches. Remember to remove

the pins as you get close to them to prevent them from bending and needles from breaking.

5. **Press**—After stitching, press the seam allowance toward the border.

6. **Replicate**—Use the same method to do the remaining opposite sides of the borders.

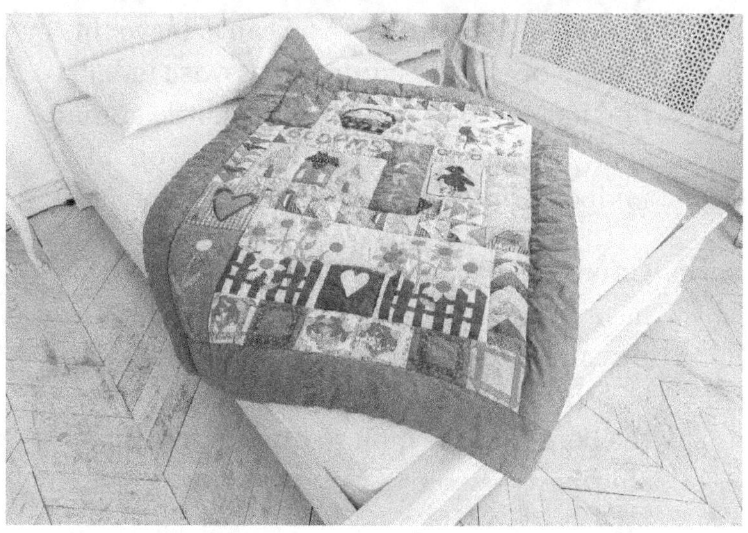

Chapter Summary

In this chapter, we learned how to do sashes and borders. Here are some key points from the chapter:

- Sashes and borders help to accentuate your central design.

- When using blocks, always keep your sashes and borders within the same size of the block.

- Always press the seam allowance toward the border.

- Don't leave your sashes and borders plain; quilt some designs.

Now that you can quilt and tie up the project with beautiful borders, let's try a Christmas special.

Chapter Thirteen: Free-Motion Quilting Christmas Special

What You Need:

1. Red fabric for the external layer.

2. White fabric for the bedding.

3. White threads.

Steps:

1. **Prepare Your Quilt Sandwich**—By now, you are probably already an expert at basting. Through practice, you have mastered the art of making your fabric taught without stretching it and choosing the right batting for your sandwich. Here is another opportunity to perfect your skills.

2. **Now Prepare Your Quilting Machine—** Clean and oil your machine, install your darning foot, and lower your feed dogs. Set the stitch length to zero. You are now the boss— and you deserve it.

3. **Prepare Your Holly Design**—Christmas is the season to celebrate and spread some love and cheer. The holly design includes berries

and spiky leaves. The best thing to do is draw the design on a piece of paper first, so you can practice a bit beforehand. Drawing on paper first will help you internalize the design. You also get an opportunity to visualize how your final project will look.

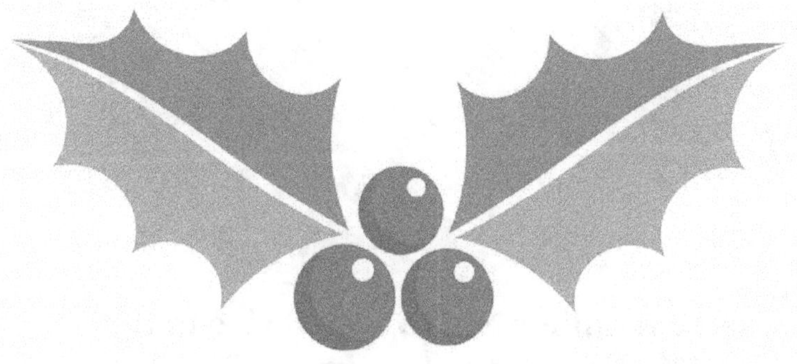

4. **Slowly Start Quilting the Design on Your Quilt Sandwich**—Quilting a holly design is much like stitching the pebbles and the star. You have had practice and are ready to make the best holly design you have ever made. You can be confident that this will be your best project yet. Slowly start by meandering before stitching the berries. Once done, you can stitch the spiky leaf. The secret to achieving those sharp spikes lies in slowing down, so you can have time to focus and begin the curved part of the leaf. The spikes are similar to the stars; you can enjoy the fruits of time spent practicing.

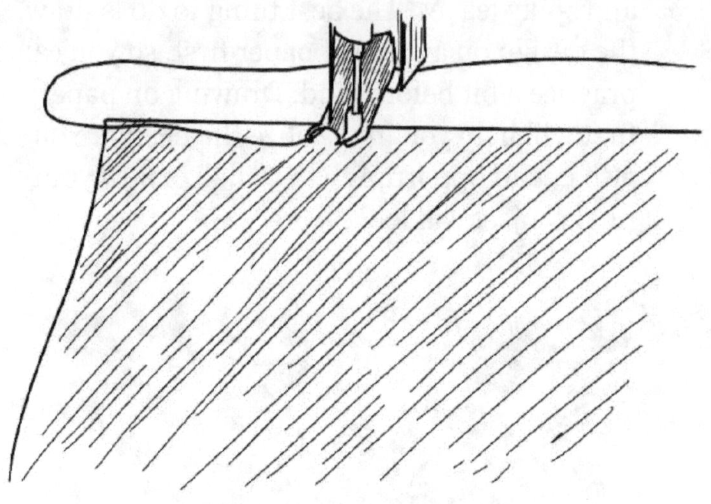

5. **Remember Not to Sew Twice in the Middle of Your Design**—Although you may be tempted to sew twice, resist the urge and keep your design clean and elegant. It will also help to keep your fabric undamaged.

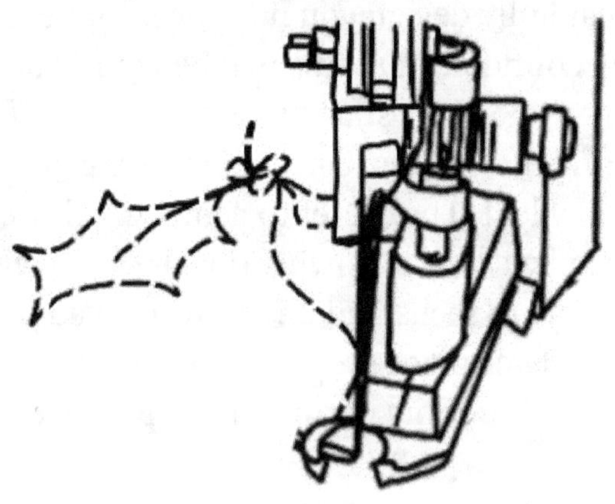

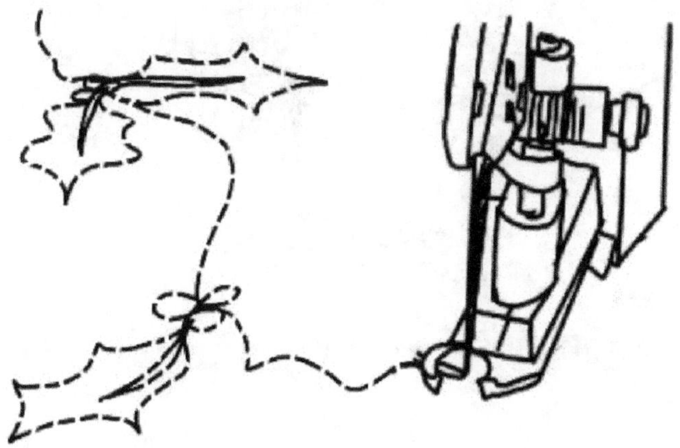

6. **Use Fillers**—If you find that you have made some small mistakes in your design, you can add some fillers. You can use them to hide any unbalanced areas and keep the focus off any part of the quilt you do not want to draw attention to.

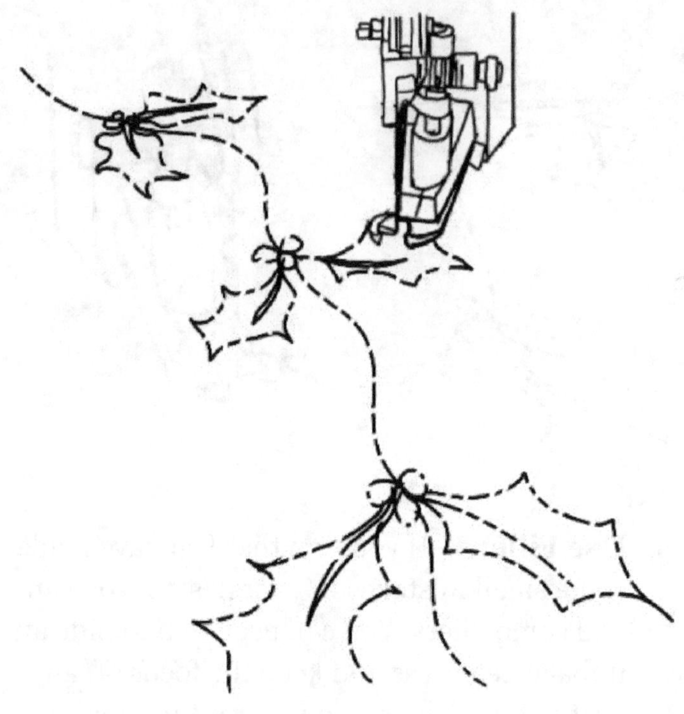

7. **Secure It by Double-Stitching the Last Two Stitches**—You do not want that beautiful holly design to start running before you even get an opportunity to show it off. To keep everything secure, double-stitch the last two stitches to keep them well-anchored.

8. **Gift Away**—This quilt can be the perfect gift for any loved one. You could even stitch your name and the names of those you want to give to on the quilt, making it more personalized. Gifting quilts will also give you an opportunity to show off what you have achieved so far.

9. **Appreciate the Feedback**—Quilters are a self-conscious group, and often, their own worst critics. Enjoy and appreciate the compliments. You need to realize that those around you genuinely appreciate the hard work you put into the quilt and likely won't notice minor mistakes. If they do, it's the last of their concern. Take in the compliments and let them motivate you to take up bigger projects. You could even get orders and start making money.

Table Runner Project

Now that you have given others something for Christmas, how about something for yourself—or if you are a giver, for someone else. You can use this project to hone your skills and gain some experience. Practice makes perfect, and what better way to keep practicing than through interesting projects. This time, let's try making a table runner.

What You Need:

1. Quilt fabric.

2. Cotton batting.

3. Cotton thread, 100%.

4. Safety pins.

5. Sewing needles.

6. Monofilament thread (optional).

7. Masking tape.

Steps

1. **Bast the Sandwich**—By now, you are getting the hang of basting, but a quick reminder never hurts. Take your fabric and lay it out on a clean and flat surface, then tape the back to the surface. Remember that the key is to have it taut but not stretched. Place your batting on top of the fabric, but do not tape it. You would then put the top fabric on the batting and smoothen the sandwich. You can now begin placing your pins one or two inches apart.

2. An important tip is to pin away from seam allowances and allow for seams to be quilted in the ditch or along a design line. You do not want your walking foot to catch on the safety pins. Also, not having to remove safety pins along the way will save you a lot of time.

3. **Set Up the Sewing Machine**—Install your quilting foot, thread the machine, and set the needle down function. Having the needle down is like giving you an extra hand, and help is welcome. Also, adjust your tension setting. You are now ready for the actual work.

4. **Ditch Quilting**—Remember that this is sewing on the lower side of a seam and as close as possible. You have to manoeuvre the sandwich. With ditch quilting, you have to be

keen on seeing where the needle pierces through the fabric. Since the stitches are close to the edge without hitting it and stitch lines are straight, your work is to keep the eye on the needle. Again, remember to sew at your speed. You should not take ditch quilting as a race— what you need is control. Use whatever speed that allows you to feel in control.

5. **Stabilize the Quilt**—A way to stabilize your quilt is by quilting the line that lies closest to the quilt's center, running North and South. Next, quilt the ditch that is either the centermost or running East and West. Since it's a table runner, you may find that some of the lines are borders.

6. **Fill in the Ditch**—Fill in with the ditch quilting, working out to the edge from the central lines. You can then flip your sandwich at 180 degrees and start again from the center.

7. **Quilt Around the Outside Edge**—You need to make a stitching line around the edge, outside of the sandwich. Keep it at less than ¼ inches, so you ensure it's within the seam allowance. The binding will cover this later.

8. **Use Fillers**—Free-motion quilting and ditch quilting use different eye positions, and you are better off finishing with ditch quilting before starting free-motion. You do not have to switch back and forth. I suggest doing filler designs

last because they tend to draw up the quilt. Choose a filler design—stippling is a good bet—but do not limit yourself.

9. **Distribute Your Quilting**—Your table runner may be a bit long, depending on your table, but ensure that you quilt as evenly as you can over it. Remember that quilted areas tend to draw up heavily.

Chapter Summary

You should now have confidence in your ever-improving free-motion quilting skills and can produce basic designs. Gifting quilts that you made by yourself is a major milestone and needs a celebration! I am certain that you now have a good understanding of your machine and have created a rapport with it by now.

From here, the sky's the limit. Keep practicing, keep quilting, and keep finishing those projects, no matter how bad you may think they are.

Inspiring Gallery of Finished Quilts

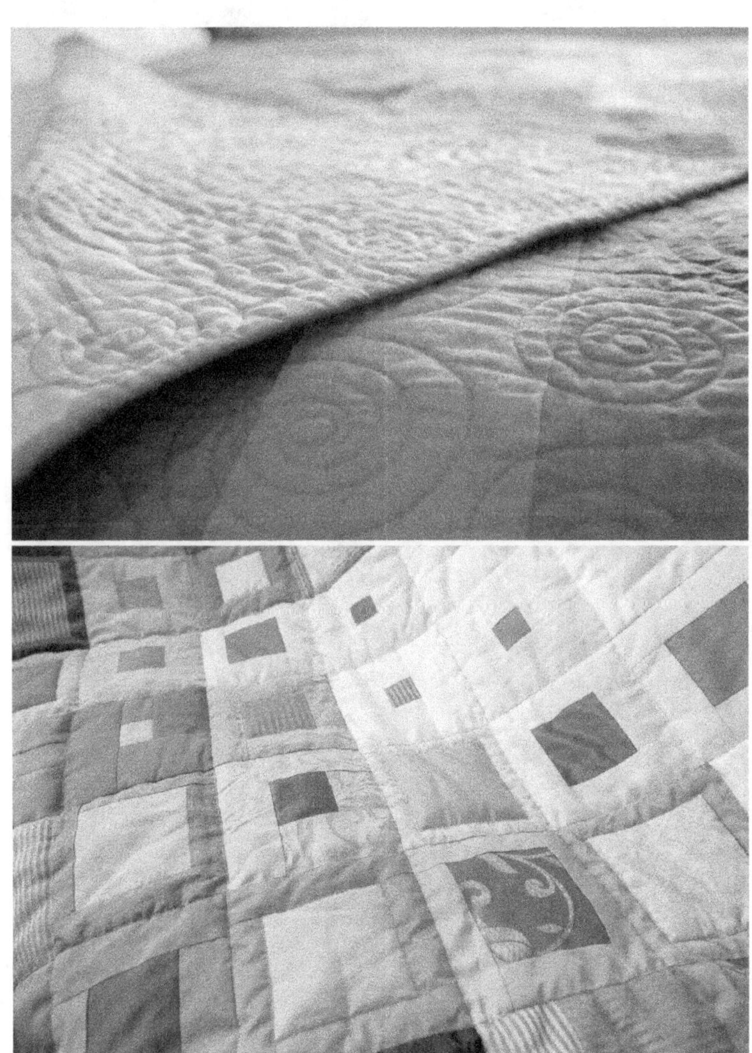

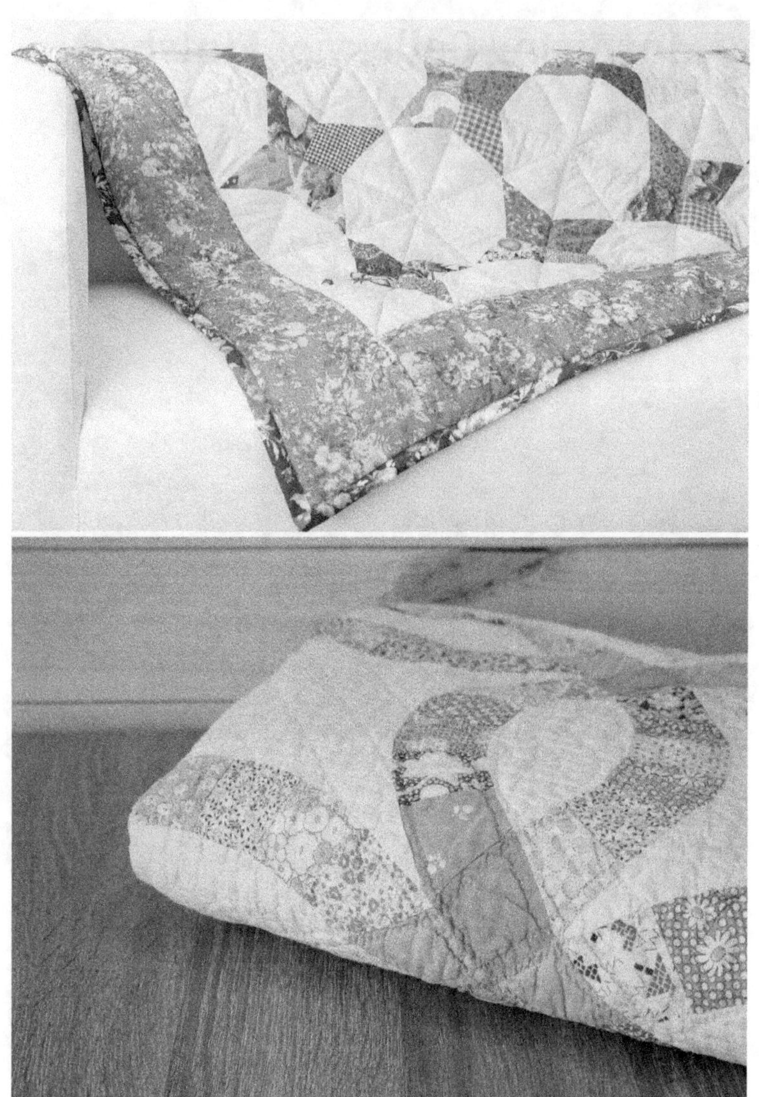

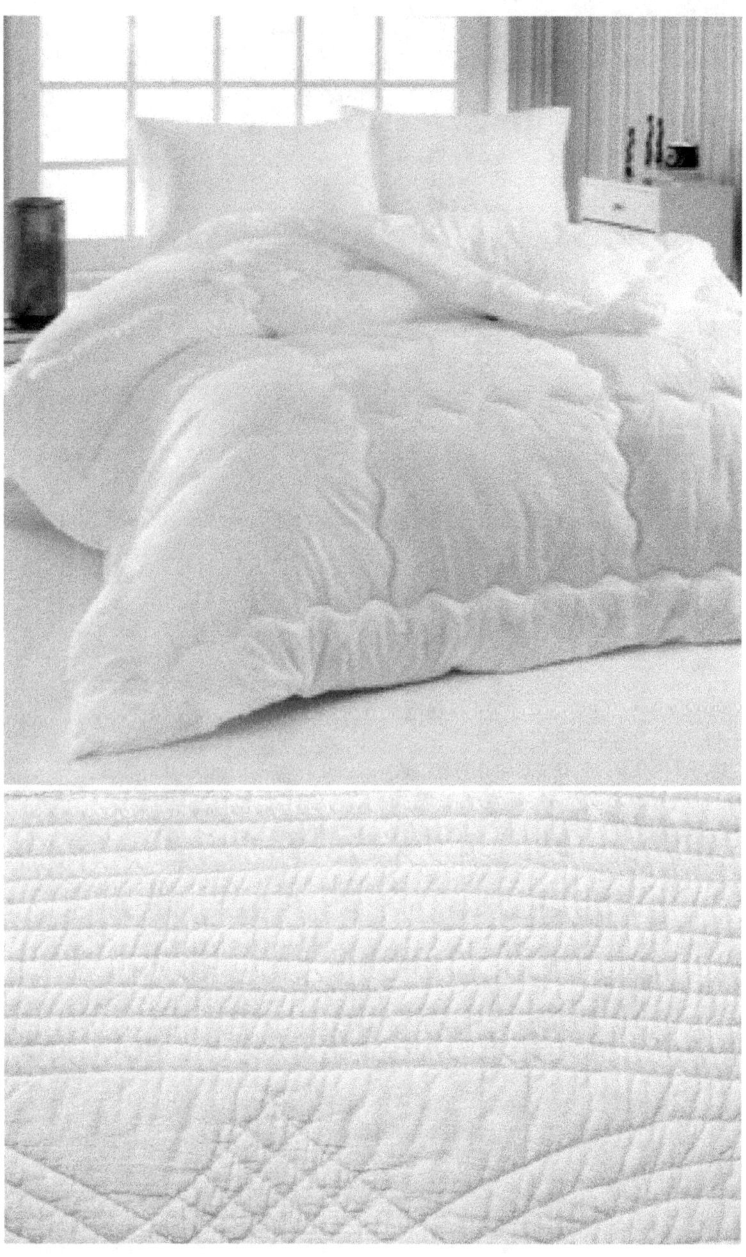

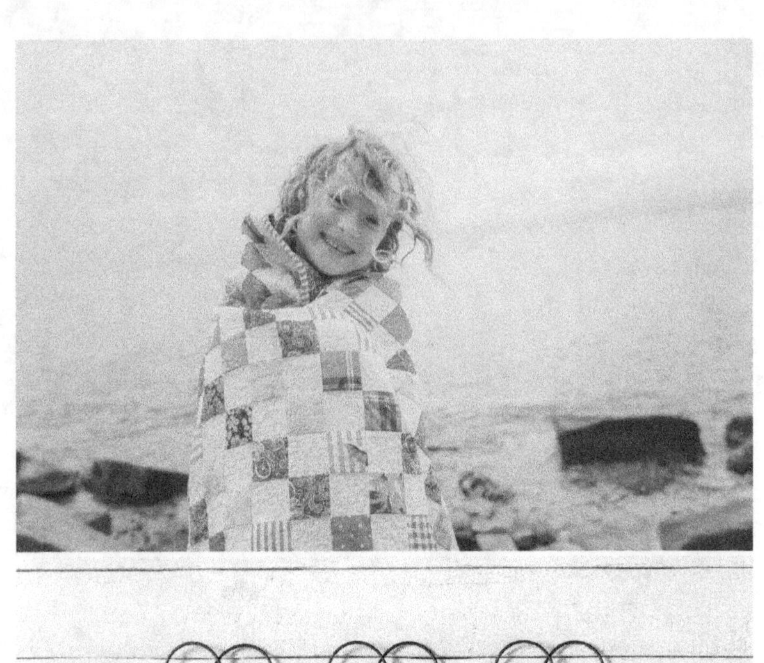

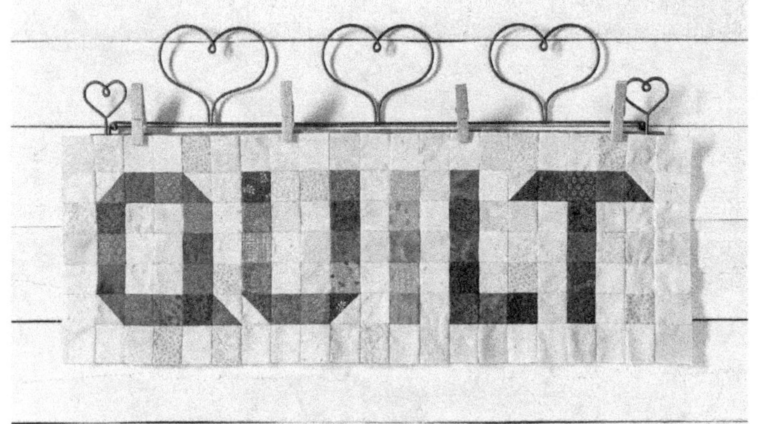

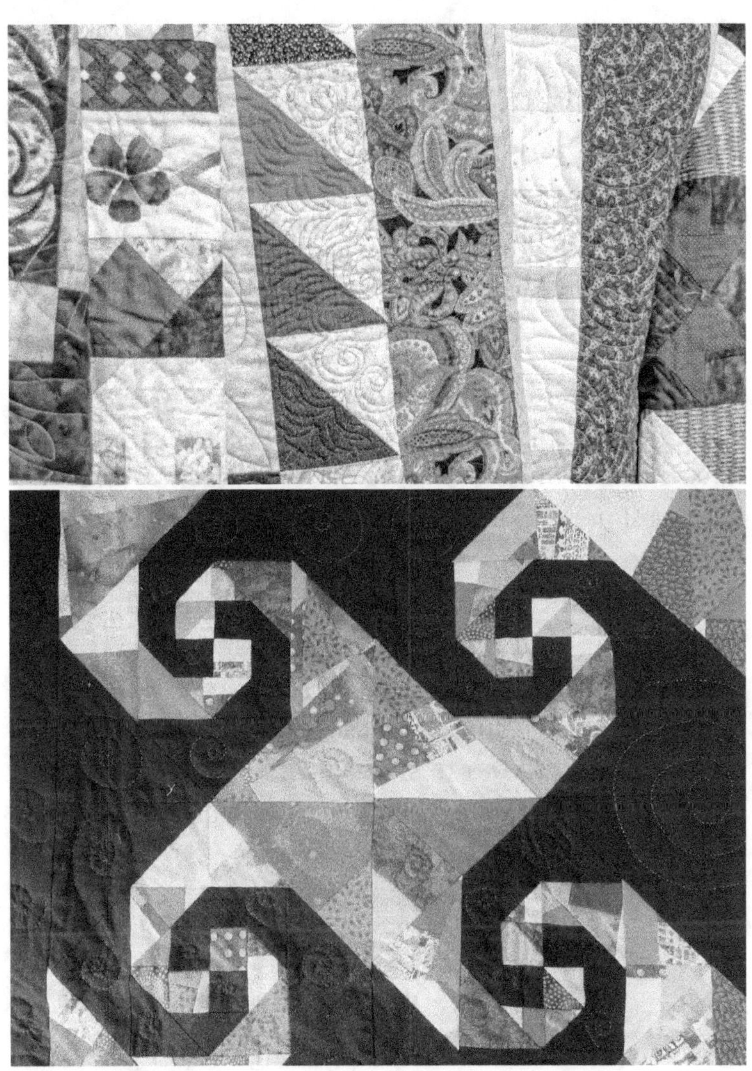

Final Words

The hardest part of any journey is the beginning, and they say, "The journey of a thousand miles starts with a single step." You have come so far already, and if you are here, you deserve a pat on the back.

Throughout this journey, you have gained a wealth of knowledge on free-motion quilting. You now have a better understanding of your machine and what you need to make your quilting experience enjoyable. You can choose your thread and pair it with an appropriate needle, in addition to setting up your machine for quilting. Your basting skills have grown considerably with practice, and you can certainly begin a project. You can make, mark, stitch, and complete any of your designs. From now on, gifting will be easier because, no matter the season, you can quilt something personal for someone.

Quilting is not just any other activity. Quilting is a way of life and antidote from life's stresses and sicknesses; it is a place of peace and enjoyment. Mastering free-motion quilting is a goal that gives much joy, as long as you are willing to put in the effort. Allocate time each day. Fifteen or twenty minutes each day will have you creating masterpieces soon enough. Like all important things in life, you have to commit.

Above all, enjoy the process, appreciate every stitch, and celebrate any finished project—no matter how small. As you quilt freely and grow continually, may your bobbin never run out of thread!

Intermediate Guide to Free-Motion Quilting

Introduction

Welcome to the Intermediate Guide to Free-Motion Quilting. Completing the Beginners Guide to Free-Motion Quilting was a great feat. It was the right thing to do to advance your Free-Motion Quilting skills: Congratulations!

In this book, you will learn advanced Free-Motion Quilting techniques and do some serious Quilting projects. All of these projects will boost your confidence, increase your level of expertise, and push you a step further until you become a pro. Does this sound simple? Not at all. You'll have to combine creativity with commitment to get there.

This book will teach you how to stitch in a ditch, how to do echoing and stippling, how to design a baby quilt, and how to create paisley on quilts. After you complete reading this book, you'll understand strip-pieced contemporary chevron quilts, modern X designs, and shattered frame quilts, as well as how to create them in the comfort of your home.

Here is the book that will turn you to a pro Free-Motion Quilter!

Chapter One:
FMQ Advanced Doodling

Approaches to drawing or sketching are not what they were a few years ago. Demand for advanced doodling is so high that everyone needs to up their skills to compete successfully. Still, creativity is the backbone of every amazing design out there. Creativity is key but you need to learn some advanced doodling techniques to birth your creative ideas. In this chapter, you get to see some advanced techniques of doodling, and a few creative doodling projects that you can create. To start, let's design a quilt, doodle our name on it, and spice it up with some lovely flowers.

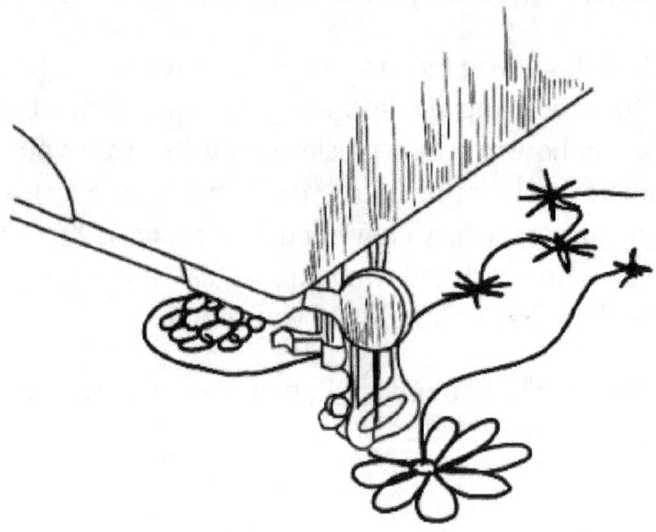

Required Materials:

- A pair of Scissors

- Pieces of Fabric

- Some Threads

- Needle (based on the threads)

- A Quilting Machine

Instructions to follow to make the Quilt:

Step 1. Prepare the Fabric: Decide how you want the Quilt to look like and cut the fabric to shape.

Step 2. Ready the Quilting Machine: Needle the machine and fix the thread. Feel free to use any thread you like but make sure the color works with the fabric.

Step 3. Set the fabric on the Machine: Locate the point to start quilting and place it directly under the needle.

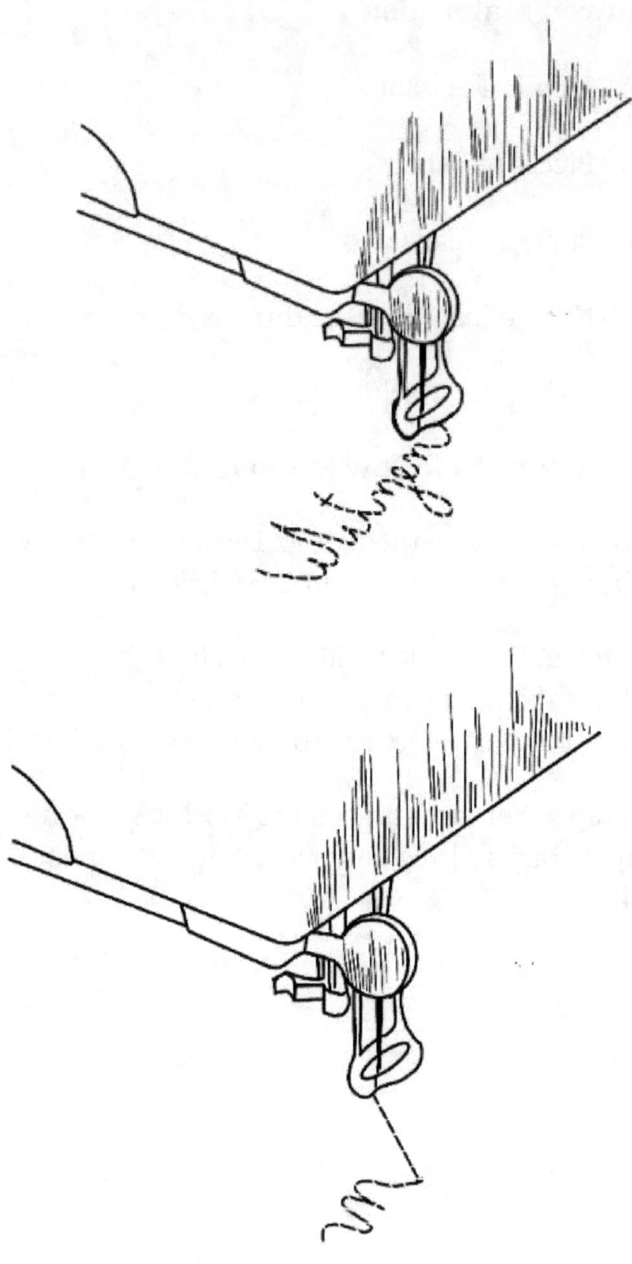

Step 4. Doodle Your Name: Start with your first name before you doodle your second name. Doodle a few circles to highlight your name. Randomize the size of the circles to make them look natural and charming.

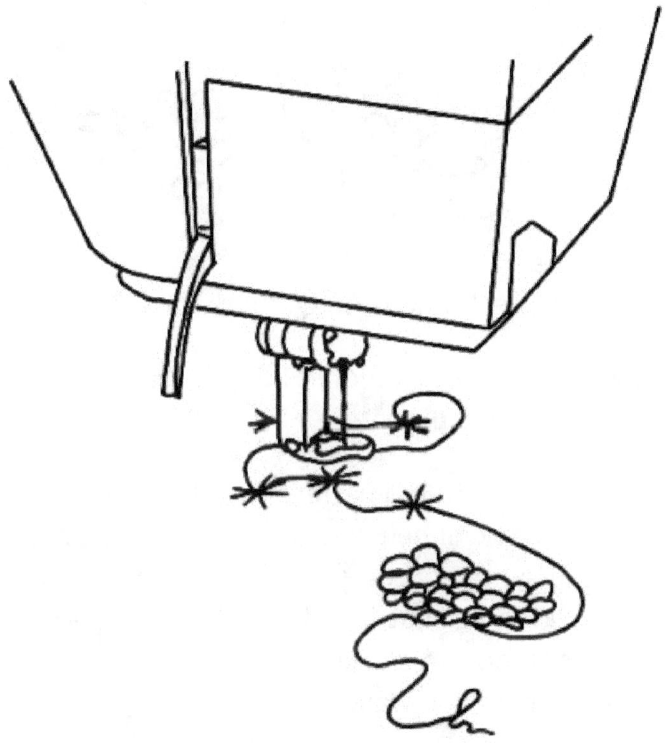

Step 5. Add the Flowers: Doodle some lovely flowers and leaves on the fabric to make it irresistible and appealing.

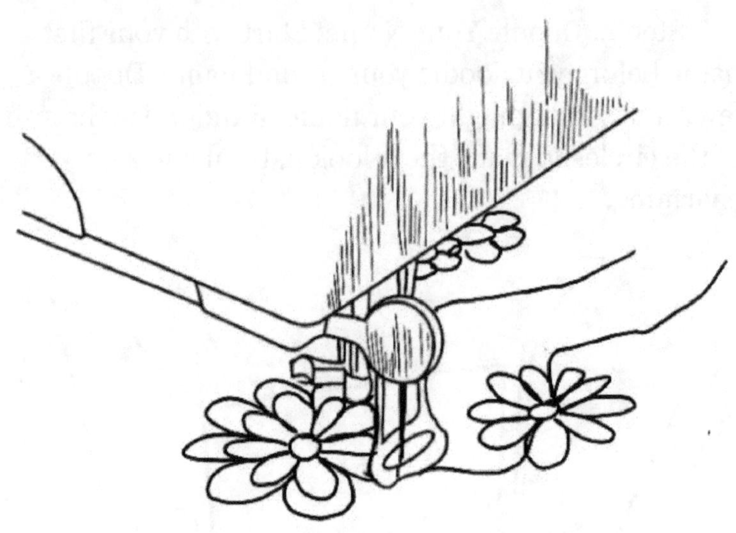

Quilting Techniques All Quilters Must Master

Here are a few techniques all quilters must master to advance their skills.

1. Rotary Cutting: Learning how to do this perfectly can help you do away with the boring time-sapping process of designing templates or marking and cutting of each layer of fabric. Use rotary tools to cut several layers of fabric as quickly as you want.

2. Seam Allowance: Learn how to visualize both 5/8" seam allowance for garments and 1/4" seam allowance for quilts without having to measure them all the time. Again, with constant practice, you'll get it right but don't forget that inaccurate seam allowance could

frustrate the whole project. Continue measuring to ensure accuracy.

3. Piecing Techniques: Get used to strip piecing if you want to finish your projects in record time. The technique helps you sew several pieces of fabric together to form strips, a quilt block lookalike. Just follow the pattern you're using to create a quilt block and you'll get it right.

4. Designing a Quilt Sandwich: A quilt sandwich is designed before sewing can start. Yes, you already know that but do you know how to baste it? No worries. Here is how to use basting technique to design a quilt sandwich.

    - Ready the quilt backing but make sure it is three or four inches larger than the quilt. Again, let the backing go inward before you begin sewing.

    - Pin the quilt down on its right side over your work surface.

    - Lay the batting directly in the middle of the backing but ensure that both are equally sized. Remove bumps, loose threads, and trim any long threads around the seam allowance.

    - Baste the quilt sandwich. Feel free to baste it with long stitches or simply use your sewing machine. You'll need to pin the

layers if you decide to baste it with your
sewing machine.

5. Pressing Techniques: Pressing, not ironing, is
    another technique you just have to master.
    Press your quilt blocks as soon as you design
    them. Pressing will enhance your patchwork
    and keep your quilt blocks fitted and neat.

6. Appliqué: Learn how to add unique final
    touches to your quilt. Feel free to use fusible,
    reverse, and freezer quilt appliqué to beautify
    your quilts.

    - Freezer Appliqué: Pick the design you want
      to use and trace it onto kitchen freezer
      paper and use the design to cut your fabric.
      You'll need to stitch the design on the quilt.

    - Reverse Appliqué: Use the reverse method
      to create a unique visual effect. How? Cut a
      piece of fabric and sew the design under it.
      People won't see the real design but they
      will see its reflection.

    - Fusible Appliqué: Attach the design to your
      fabric with a fusible web; you'll need a
      significant amount of heat to run the
      process.

Constant practice is what you need to master
these techniques. If things do not turn out the way you

want, intensify your practice. You'll get used to the techniques and improve.

How to Make a Crazy Quilt Block

Crazy Quilt blocks come with plenty of embellishments and they are quite easy to make. With little actual measuring, you can create these super exciting blocks that will make up the quilts to beautify your lovely homes. Fantastic! Here is how to make a Crazy Quilt Block.

Required Materials:

- Muslin

- Rotary cutter

- Cutting mat

- Iron

- Ruler

- Sewing machine

- Basic sewing gear

- Many fabric scraps

Follow these simple steps to make your own Crazy Quilt Block

Step 1. Prepare Your Fabric Scraps: Carefully consider the size of your design before you cut your fabric scraps. Most designs use 2" cut-to-size fabric scraps but make sure your scraps have enough space around them. Don't worry about the space. You can trim the scraps before you start joining the pieces together. Cut a big scrap of sticky stabilizer and place your fabric scraps in its center. Make sure that the sticky stabilizer fits the hoop of your machine.

Step 2. Cut Your Muslin to Size: Determine the size you want your Quilt to be and add your seam allowance. Better still, cut your Muslin square to 12 1/2" while your seam allowance is 1/4" to have a perfect square of 12" Crazy Quilt Blocks. Again, it all depends on the size you want.

Step 3. Trim the Center Square: Be creative as you add some fun angles to your Center Square. Still, make sure you trim along a straight line. Use your ruler to mark the areas to trim. Pin the trimmed piece face-up on your Muslin square.

Step 4. Stitch the Muslin Square: Don't forget to stay within the 1/4" seam allowance as you zigzag switch the Muslin square. Iron the square consistently to make it look nice and straighten its edges.

Step 5. Join the Fabric Scraps: Stylishly pin the strips on either side of the Muslin square and stitch. Run the process until you are done with the second layer. Again, remember to stitch the 1/4" seam allowance before you cover the piece or stitch the edges.

Step 6. Trim the Muslin Square: Flip the piece on your cutting mat, trace the excess piece with your ruler, and cut with your rotary cutter. Again, make sure you cut all the excess fabrics. Next, zigzag switch-stitch all the edges.

Step 7. Add Finishing Touches: Feel free to adorn your Crazy Quilt Block with buttons, beads, or any other embellishments.

How to Make a Photo Quilt

Feel free to print your favorite photographic images on your fabrics and the process is so simple that you can create your own photo quilt at the comfort of your home. Here is how you can make it.

Required Materials:

- White Cotton Fabric (2 Yards)

- Batting 36 × 48

- Bubble Jet Set 2000

- Bubble Jet Rinse

- Cardboard for templates

- A large lasagna pan

- A pencil

- Drawing paper

- A computer, inkjet printer, and printer paper

- Freezer paper

- A digital camera

- A sewing machine

- Large piece of thick felt

- Disappearing ink pen

- Sewing accessories such as thread, scissors, pins, ironing board, seam ripper, iron, healing mat, rotary cutter, and cutting guide

- Quilt thread

Follow these simple steps to make your own Photo Quilt:

Step 1. Select Your Images and Fabrics: Take your time to select the images and fabrics you want to use for your Photo Quilt.

Step 2. Ready the Images and Fabrics: Wash and iron the fabrics you just purchased. Cut to your freezer paper and white cotton fabric. While the paper is shaped to 8 1/2 × 11 sheets, the fabric is slightly larger.

Use the Bubble Jet Set 2000 to soak the white fabric for five minutes before you dry it with a towel. Place the freezer paper on the ironing board, make sure it is not lying on its shiny side, and place your treated fabric on it. Use a hot iron to press thoroughly to bond the fabric with the freezer paper.

Carefully trim excess fabric and run it through the inkjet printer. Do some test prints to see if the color alignment is perfect. Allow the fabric to dry properly before you rinse it in the diluted Bubble Jet Rinse to avoid color bleeding.

Step 3. Sketch the Pattern and Cut Your Pieces: Draw a pattern of the Photo Quilt you intend to make and use it as a sewing guide. Cut the pieces and add 1/4 seam allowance before you join the fat quarters. Use the printed fabric to make the circles or a simple standout design. Use the clear cutting guide, rotary cutter, and the self-healing mat to cut the squares to shape. Use the disappearing ink pen to trace the circles before you cut with scissors.

Cut the pattern from cardboard, press its curved edge on the seam allowance, and use a zigzag stitch to join it to the squares.

Step 4. Get the Big Picture with Wall Felt: Attach the cotton fabric to the wall to see how the Photo Quilt is getting to shape. Should there be no Wall Felt, use pins to hang the Quilt to the wall. You can alternate circles and squares to harmonize colors and patterns.

Step 5. Stack Blocks for Sewing: Stack the circles and squares to three layers of rows and sew them.

Step 6. Add Backing and Batting: Cut your backing and batting fabric but make sure it is larger than the regular Quilt top. Baste the three layers from the middle and of the Quilt and space the rows of basting 4-inches apart.

Step 7. Sew the Quilt: Run the sewing from the center to the outward parts of the quilt. You can use the disappearing ink to mark lines on the quilt to determine the sewing path.

How to Turn Old Jeans to Quilts

Old and worn out jeans do not benefit you if they are stacked in your wardrobe. They take up space or litter your wardrobe. No worries! You can use your old ripped, grass-stained, and zippered jeans as well as their denim pockets to make lovely Quilts. The process of turning old jeans to Quilts is so simple that you can do it in your home! A few steps and you are good to go.

Required Materials

- A few pairs of Jeans (between 3 and 5)

- A pair of Scissors

- Many Stick Pins

- Thread

- A flat Bed Sheet

- A Sewing Machine

Follow these simple steps to turn your old jeans to Quilts:

Step 1. Ready Your Jeans: Split each pair of jeans from the middle seam through the crotch to the two back pockets. Cut off the seam to open the legs. Should you need to use other parts of the jeans, cut them out. The number of jeans to use depends on the size of Quilt you want to make.

Step 2. Trim Jeans to Workable Pieces: Stylishly cut the jeans to pieces that you can sew on the machine. Remember that the fabric can cause you some sewing issues if they are not well stretched.

Step 3. Fit the Pieces: Carefully fit the pieces. Create room for at least 1 inch overlap to ease sewing and don't forget to square off the edges. Feel free to add your favorite pocket but you'll need to create some space between the pocket and the edge.

Step 4. Join the Pieces: Pin the already laid out pieces but don't forget that they must overlap one inch. Fold the overlapping part and join the pieces together, one after the other.

Step 5. Sew the Pieces: Some people say a dark-blue thread is perfect for sewing this Quilt but feel free to use any color you want.

Step 6. Prepare the Backing: Use a colored flat bed sheet for the Quilt. The color depends on how you want the quilt to look like. But I'll suggest you to go for a navy or a dark-blue flat bed sheet. Make sure all the sides are wide up to 6 or 8 inches. Spread the sheet and stretch it to smoothen its wrinkles and rough edges before you place the jean in its center.

Step 7. Square the Quilt: Cut the flat bed sheet according to the pattern of the jeans. Trim excess chunks from the edges to make the shape straight and fit.

Step 8. Join the Backing: Fold the edges of the flat bed sheet into that of the quilt. Check if both can work together or you'll have to do some trimmings. Pin both on their four sides and sew them together.

Step 9. Add Final Touches: Feel free to personalize your quilt by including the date you made it or some sorts of expressions.

Chapter Summary

- Demand for quilts is on the increase and creativity is the backbone of every amazing quilt out there.

- Be patient and committed enough to design your favorite quilts because some quilts are hard to create.

You're learning so fast, good. In the next chapter, you will learn raw edge applique. See you there.

Chapter Two: Raw Edge Appliqué

Raw edge appliqué quilts are beautiful, charming, and attractive. They are quilts you really don't want to miss. Sure, you can design your own raw edge appliqué quilt in the comfort of your home but you'll need to up your creativity a bit. Yes, creating a fancy raw edge appliqué quilt could be a little bit hard unless you learn the process. No worries. I'll teach you how you can use raw edge appliqué to improve your stitching designs and all you need to do to create your appliqué motif. No more talking! Here is how to create the raw edge appliqué.

Required Materials

- Appliqué cloth

- An already sewed garment

- Iron-on adhesive

- All-purpose polyester thread in a matching color

- Tweezers

- A pair of scissors

- Fine safety pins

Follow these simple steps to design your own raw edge appliqué quilt:

Step 1: Cut a piece of your appliqué cloth. This cloth should be an inch longer than your design. Cut a piece of iron-on adhesive. Make it be in the same size with your appliqué cloth piece.

Step 2: Make the iron-on adhesive paper be in line with the appliqué cloth. The cloth and gummy side of the paper should be aligned. Iron the design with high heat.

Step 3: Use a pair of scissors to cut out your design.

Step 4: Remove the adhesive paper. You can make use of tweezers to remove the paper from the fragile part of the fabric.

Placing the Motif

Step 1: Hang the garment on a hook in order to form the best type of appliqué placement. Drag the motif about, and endeavor to try several angles before choosing your own.

Step 2: Once you find the angle you like best for the placement of the motif, remove all the useless parts and pin your motif to the garment.

Attaching the Motif

Step 1: Attach the motif to the garment. Iron it with high heat from the top corner right side. To maintain your intended shape, place a tailor's ham under the garment.

Step 2: Stitch it closely to the edge and around the appliqué motif.

Tips for Sewing Motifs

Step 1: Employ an edgestitch foot to preserve a steady space between the raw edge and sewing. Join the edge guide with the raw edge of the appliqué when you are stichting. Then, change the position of the needle to the right or left to keep the sewing distance.

Step 2: Anytime you are not stitching, place your sewing machine to either needle up to make room for easy manipulation of the fabric. It will accelerate your stitching

Step 3: Modify the length of the sewing. A shorter sewing length will give you room to sew the tight corners and make the motif equal.

Simple Appliqué Using Straight Stitch

You have been using straight-stitch for appliqué regularly in your workplace. The fact is that there are no special machine settings needed for this stitching; it's a simple day to day stitching technique.

In order to do simple applique using straight, there are two methods. They are regular stitch and free motion stitching. The regular stitch will help you to work on larger appliqué shapes with little tight curves or corners. In a case where the appliqué is tiny it is better to use free motion stitching.

Free motion stitching involves fitting a hopping foot on your stitching machine and selecting the free motion setting.

Required Materials

- Regular Foot

- Thread

- Stitching Machine

Follow these simple steps to stitch your applique quilt:

Step 1: Thread the sewing machine using colored thread or any thread if choice. Make sure that you place the medium stitch length at default length.

Step 2: Let the feed dogs be up and place your appliqué in the right side up position, then tack into place.

Step 3: Gently sew near the edges of each appliqué piece, turn the cloth where seen it fit.

To stitch appliqué using free motion straight stitch:

Step 1: Let your sew machine be set at *free motion*. You could also set the stitch length to Zero. This looks easier.

Step 2: Let your feed dogs be at the downward position

Step 3: Sew with either color or contrasting thread.

Step 4: Set your appliqué up at the right hand side of cloth, then pin into place.

Step 5: Gently sew close to the side of each appliqué piece. Make sure you tacitly manipulate the fabric in order to get the curves and corners right.

Zigzag sewing

Zigzag sewing is so dynamic that it can be used to create many effects, and it only depends on the sewing length you prefer for your zigzag stitch. This depends on the type of method you want and the type of design available or needed sewing.

Step 1: Place your appliqué up on the right side of your base of your cloth, then tack it with a pin.

Step 2: use a zigzag foot on your machine to thread the machine with any thread of choice.

Step 3: Raise the feed dogs a bit.

Step 4: Position your choiced stitch length and gently sew it near the side of your appliqué.

Satin stitch – A Type of Zigzag Stitch

This stitch is not different from zigzag, although it is placed at a short stitch length. It is a wonderful stitch because it makes your appliques look attractive and lovely. It can be used as a decorative feature.

Required Materials

- Appliqué cloth

- Thread

- Sharp scissors

- Fine pins

Instructions

Follow these simple steps to design your own satin stitch

Step 1: Place your appliqué up on the right side of your cloth, then tack it with a pin.

Step 2: Let the feed dogs be kept up.

Step 3: Use a zigzag foot on your sewing machine to thread with any color of your own. Let the length be set to a short or medium stitch. Then, you can tactfully sew it close to the edges of your appliqué.

Blanket Stitch.

Blanket stitch is another very important zigzag stitch. To do blanket stitch, the sew machine is positioned to sew in a very complex way than merely side to side. This stitch allows fast and stress free addition of your appliqué pieces. Usually, it is used to make a country or cottage-style applique.

Instructions

Follow these simple steps to design your Blanket Stitch

Step 1: Place your appliqué up on the right side of your cloth, then tack it with a pin.

Step 2: apply the useful foot on your sewing machine to thread the machine with toning or contrasting thread.

Step 3: Let the feed dogs be kept up.

Step 4: Place your stitch length either small or medium width.

Step 5: Tactfully see the fabric towards the edges of your appliqué.

Step 6: Try to usually make small pivots at the start of the sewing to maintain the smooth curves.

Decorative Stitches.

Many of the newly developed sewing machines contain a range of decorative stitches. These machines are expensive but they are easy to use. These decorative sewing are used to get a fine effect with appliqué. The major problem with this stitch is deciding the type and quantity of thread to use. You can use any thread as long as it will produce needed effect. To choose a thread you must determine the weight of the thread and composition of the thread

Required Materials

- Appliqué cloth

- Thread

- Sharp scissors

- Fine pins

Instructions

Follow these simple steps to use decorative stitches

Step 1: use a thick thread to give fast protection.

Step 2: Use light thread to protect less area.

Step 3: Choose a good thread because the thread you select affects the look of your work.

Step 4: Stitch softly along the line of the fabric to maintain your decoration.

How to Design a Fusible Raw Edge Applique Quilts

Fusible raw edge applique is the freest and quickest quilting technique. Most beginners develop their skills by practicing this quilting style. This method involves using fusible web and water soluble pens.

Required Materials

- Fusible web

- Water soluble pen

- Appliques

- Washable marker

- Fabric

Instructions

Follow these simple steps to design your own raw edge applique quilt.

Step 1: Sketch your project on a paper

Step 2: Move the sketch to the fabric you use for the background using a temporary marker.

Step 3: Change the method and move it to the piece of paper in the side of the fusible web, then allow some space between the pieces.

Step 5: Trim the fusible web out anyhow; put it on the fusible web templates, side down, to the wrong side of the opposite fabric.

Step 6: Trim it nearly along the lines.

Step 7: Take away the paper place at the back of the pieces.

Step 8: Position each fabric piece in an alternative way.

Step 9: Iron with a high heat to force the pieces to appear on background fabric.

How to Create Applique Without Marking the Fabric

When you don't have a water soluble marker but you urgently need to carry out a design that needs appliques.You need to apply an appliques that without marking the fabric. This method can be applied on a light color cloth. Let me explain step by step of doing this.

Step by step application of applique without marking the fabric

Step 1: if your fabric is transparent and you can see the pattern through it, iron the paper pattern, alongside the fabric that is placed on the background. Put the applique pieces on the opposite side and iron them together.

Step 2: If the fabric is not transparent, it is advisable to glue the fusible web. Employ paper Tape to gum the paper pattern on a window and gum the fabric on it. Gum the applique pieces in the corresponding places.

Applique feet

Some clear feet and open toe feet have made it possible to protect applique pieces easily because there is a clear picture of what you want to stitch and how you want to stitch it. This foot is important and recommended for both experience and upcoming quilter.

Securing the edges of the appliques – type of stitching

There are different types of stitches you can use to gum fabric on an applique piece. These may include straight, zig-zag, satin stitch or blanket stitch. You can choose any base on the project you have at hand and the design you want.

How to Start and Stop the Applique Stitching

Step 1: When using a zig zag stitch, it is good to commence it with a few micro straight stitches. Place your stitch length to 0.5 mm. Stitch just close to the edge of the applique pieces, on the fabric used for background.

Step 2: Change to the preferred zig zag stitch.

Step 3: Make sure you end the stitch with zig zag and the last stitches should be the micro straight stitches.

Step 4: If you want to stop stitching at the starting point, stitch the zig zag till it marries the zig zag at the beginning and end the stitching with the micro straight stitches

Color of Thread for Securing the Edges

There is no special thread to use for securing the edge. Your creativity and the project determine the thread color. A color that resembles the color of the applique fabric may not look attractive but a contrasting color will definitely catch the attention to the applique because it will make it look different.

There are unlimited types of thread. They include cotton, silk, polyester, invisible thread, and they come in different weights; it may be a thick thread or a fine thread.

Needles

To effectively secure the edges of the appliques, you can use the same needles for quilting and appliques. The most used needle is the Jeans needles.

However, when you are doing a baby quilt, you may use a heavy quilt other than the appliques. When you choose an appropriate needle, you will find it hard to achieve the needed result.

You can also use sharp needles, or topstitch needles, most especially when the thread is thick.

Chapter Summary

- Raw edge applique quilts are bold and beautiful but involve a lot of processes.

- To create raw edge quilts, you need to be creative. Also, a bit of endurance will be required.

In the next chapter you will learn a few echoing and stippling projects. Get to see you there!

Chapter Three:
Echoing and Stippling

Stipple quilting is quite simple if you learn to master it. Sure, some quilters, mostly beginners, find it so hard to do, get stuck, or run over the stitching lines when echoing or stippling their quilts. Trust me. I believe you know that echoing or stippling is a filler technique used in quilting but you have to steady your hands to do it perfectly to get a beautiful result. Again, pay keen attention to the thread you intend to use for the echoing or stippling exercise. Just make sure that your chosen threads contrast your fabric. No worries. I will run you through the process and you'll master the technique in no distant time. Also, in this chapter, you will learn how to do stippling drawing, how to do straight line in quilting, and how to create your own stippling embroidered quilt block. There are so many amazing things to learn. But, before then, let's run through the echoing and stippling process.

Required Materials

- A Quilt Sandwich (already quilted with a design or shape)

- Thread (different from the color of your fabric)

- Needle (based on your thread)

Instructions

Follow the simple steps below to echo your Quilt Sandwich

Step 1. Thread and needle your quilting machine.

Step 2. Lay the quilt sandwich under the machine 1/4" into your design.

Step 3. Quilt your outline but maintain fixed distance all through.

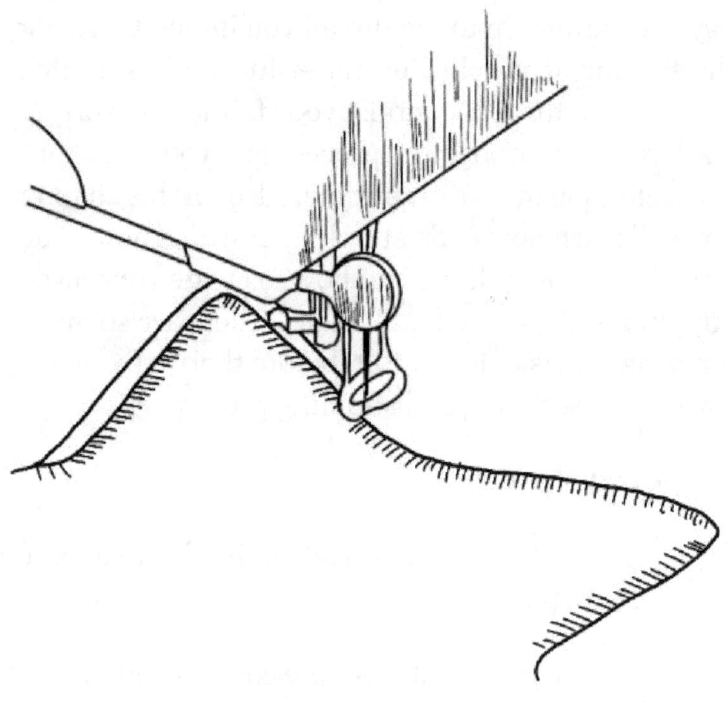

Step 4. Finish the first outline, secure and jump stitch to design another outline.

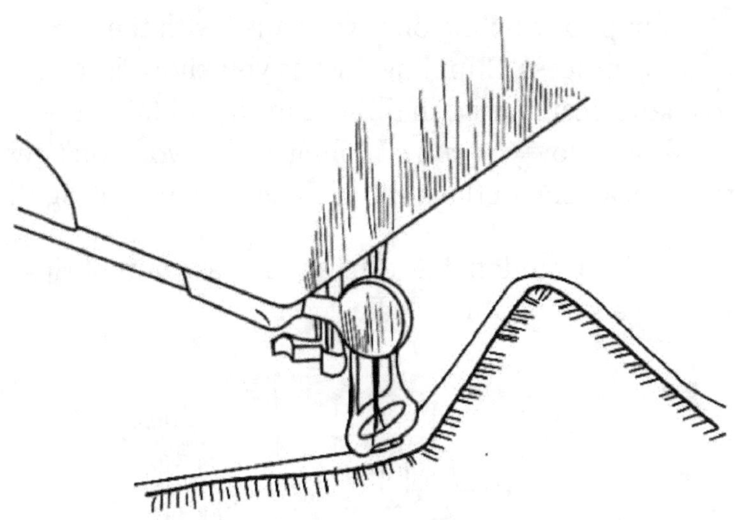

Step 5. Repeat the process until you get the
number of echoes you want.

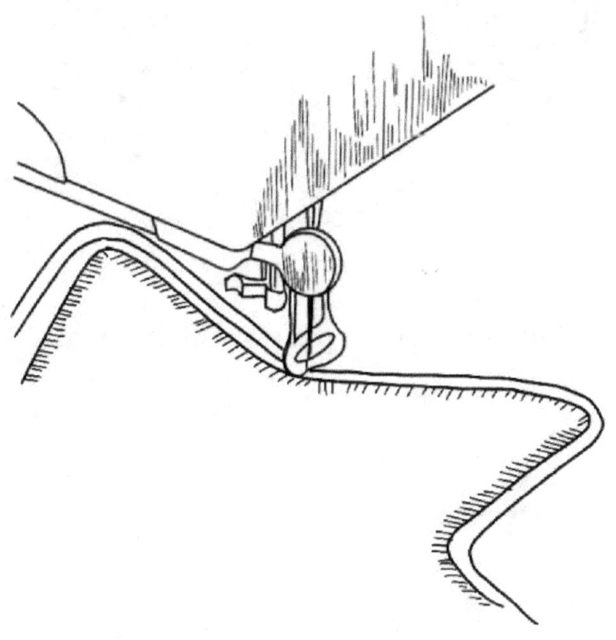

Jump to stippling once you finish with the echoing process. Stippling, just as you know, is a freehand design used in filling gaps in quilts. But be mindful of how you run stippling so that you don't get to the dead end of the quilt. Here is how to do it right.

1. Quilt random patterns as soon as your fabric gets under the needle.

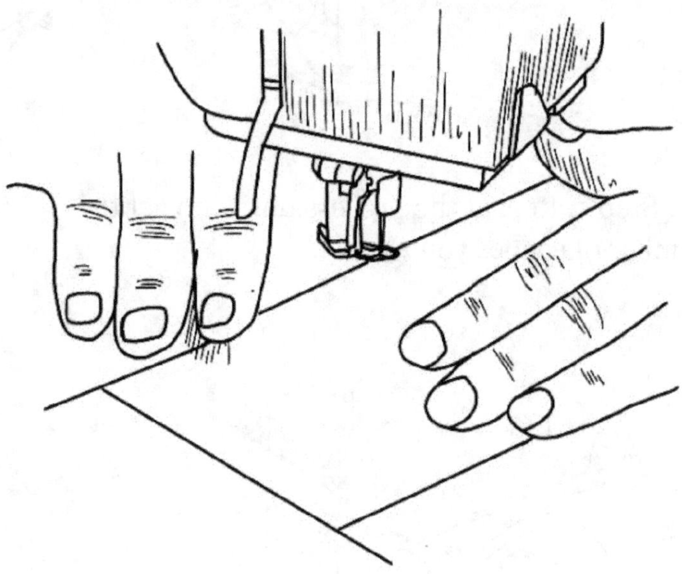

2. Maintain random patterns all through.

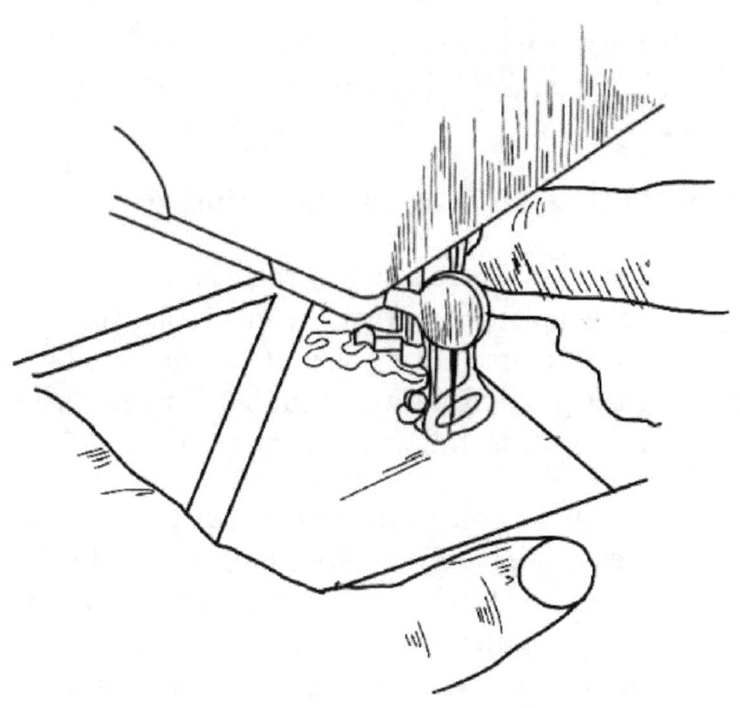

3. Don't corner your needle to avoid an empty patch on your quilt.

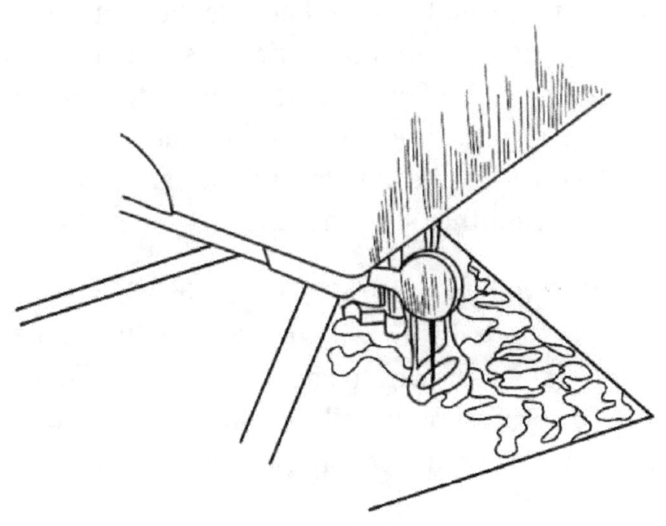

It's easy, isn't it? Sure, you'll find it useful and helpful in several quilting situations. How can I master echoing?

Tips on How You Can Master Echoing

1. Visibility: There's no way you can accurately echo quilt stitches that are not visible. Make sure the first line of your stitches stays visible. Also, properly position your quilt or you'll have issues estimating your quilting space.

    Feel free to rotate your quilt so that you can clearly see it during the echoing phase. Still, rotate it naturally and smoothly or you'll mess things up. Remember that visibility can make or mar your echoing experience. So, make sure you work things out.

2. Use the Edges: Focus more on the edges of your free-motion foot because they can aid the echoing process. First, stitch a straight line and guide yourself with the left part of the foot as you echo the line towards the practice square. Again, with the aid of the right part of the foot, stitch another straight line.

    What did you notice? Yes, the lines have consistent distance apart. Good. Still, you need to train your eyes to easily estimate the space. However, should quilting with the edges of your foot create echoing mistakes for you, adjust the distance of the last line of your stitch and your needle.

3. Draw it Clearly: The edges of your foot can work wonders but not all the time. For example, if you want to echo an object all-round, the front and back of your foot can't aid the process. Yes, this happens often but no worries. Just spread your fabric on a flat surface, mark the echoes on it, and stitch the line. Train your eyes to estimate space accurately and train your hands to maintain it if you want to master the process.

4. Embrace Your Mistakes: Don't ignore the fact that mistakes could add a beautiful dimension to your work. In one of my projects, I decided to weave my echo in and out, against the shape of the design I initially wanted to do. I stitched it my way and the whole thing turned out good and unique. So, it amounts to a waste of energy and time if you stopped stitching halfway just because you identified a few mistakes.

5. Get Started with Simple Echoing Designs: Pick echoing designs or foundational designs and practice with a baby quilt or any other simple quilt. No amount of stitching is small to up your echoing skills. But remember that echoing is a simple skill you can master in no distant time, just like piecing a quilt block or brushing your teeth. Sure, you didn't master brushing

your teeth or piecing a quilt block the very first time you tried it. So, practice echoing more if you really want to master it.

Here are a few practice steps to up your echoing and stitching skills:

Step 1. Fuse an appliqué shape in the middle of a 10" square fabric.

Step 2. Quilt round the sandwiched heart and echo the shape until you fill up the entire block.

True, you don't have to do only this practice all the time. Feel free to practice jagged plain, echo shell, Desert sand, Trippy triangles, or brain coral.

The Free-Motion Echo Quilting Foot

Exercise more control on free-motion quilting by using the free-motion echo quilting foot. Its large base serves as a surface for fabrics and it helps you maneuver the stitching process the way you want. The base is so transparent that it supports 360° visibility. Again, its foot comes with vertical, horizontal, and circular markings. These markings aid line quilting or fabric designing. So, depending on what you want to quilt, you can follow certain patterns or simply sew straight lines. Pay attention to the points below if you want to sew with the free-motion echo quilting foot.

1. Screw your presser foot to loosen the ankle. Fit the free-motion echo quilting foot in the presser and tighten it with screws.

2. Needle and thread your sewing machine.

3. Choose a straight stitch.

4. Tune the machine to Free Motion Floating to automatically drop the feed dogs.

The machine stops moving your fabric as soon as you drop the feed dogs. So, you'll need to feed it yourself.

5. Tilt up the bobbin thread and hold both threads as you sew some stitches.

6. Move the fabric smoothly and stitch at a consistent speed.

7. Stitch round the appliqué, quilting motif, and fabric pattern but ensure a uniform distance between outline and shape.

8. Stitch the second row but let there be a uniform distance between it and the previous one.

9. Repeat the process a few times to create your favorite design or pattern.

How to Make Stipple Drawings

Sure, stippling isn't just about drawings. It's using dots to create amazing pictures. So, like an expert printer, you're going to pick up your pen, do some dots, and turn them to appealing images. Did you say it's hard? No. You will master it after a few days practice. Still, you will mess up the whole thing if you press your pen too hard on the sheet of paper you're working on. Here's how to make the stipple drawings.

Required Materials

- A Sheet of Paper

- Fine Point Sharpie (Black or any color you want)

- A Ruler

- An Eraser

- A Pencil

Instructions

Follow these simple steps to make your stipple drawings.

Step 1. Print out the black-and-white drawing or design you intend to replicate.

Step 2. Sketch shapes with pencil from dark to light to know the part to stipple more. Just focus on shadings and shapes.

Step 3. Use ink to stipple the darkest areas before you work on the light areas. Don't forget you're dotting, not coloring the shade. Speed up the dotting process but don't press your pencil too hard.

Step 4. Add other details in ink and balance the shading. Don't make it too dark or too light.

Step 5. Erase border and stray pencil marks once the ink gets dry.

How to Use Stippling in Drawings

Feel free to use dots to create shadows, texture, and tone to your drawings. But, in order to create a striking effect, make the dots denser if darkness is needed or simply sparse to highlight some shapes. Still, draw simple objects often if you're still working on improving your stippling drawing skills. Ready your pencils, markers, and pens while I take you through the steps of using stippling in drawings.

Step 1. Opt for the right stippling paper. White hot-pressed papers are perfect because they are smooth and strong. They don't get blurred or absorb ink.

Step 2. Go for the right stippling drawing tools. Use pencils to stipple subtle designs. Stipple with a drawing pen once your skills improve. With a black drawing pen, you get to create crisp and dramatic designs on your white paper. But, if you must work with a pencil, choose B pencil— a soft and dark one. Also, feel free to use an artist's pen or a colored marker.

Step 3. Tap or twist your pencil to create uniform dots on your paper. But, if you're using a marker or a pen, adopt the straight-up-and-down stippling technique to create your dots on paper. Still, avoid smudging the paper or creating stray lines.

Step 4. Get started with a simple object like an egg. Draw the object and fill its shadowed areas with dots. Close the dots together where you have the darkest shadows but feel free to use few or no dots where the object reflects light.

Step 5. Use more dots to realistically shade the object.

Don't be in a hurry while using stippling in drawings because you might mess up the whole thing.

How to Create an Embroidered Quilt Block with Stippling

Here, you will learn how to design an embroidered quilt block. The block will have a floral peacock and we will stipple the peacock round. We are using the FTC-U program for this project. Here are the steps.

Step 1. Open the Design: Click the FTC-U program and tap the 'Create a New Design.' Find this icon below the opening panel. You could also use an existing design if there's one on your FTC-U program.

Next, go to the File menu to click 'Merge Stitch File' to open the file you'd like to use. Just make sure that the file works for your block. For example, choose 'Floral Animal-Peacockc.pes' if your block is 8" by 11".

Step 2. Create Outline: Click all items on the Sequence View as soon as you load your design.

Step 3. Convert Peacock to Outlines: Right-click 'All items' to open a dialog box and click 'Convert to outlines.' Conversion process could run for several seconds.

Step 4. Create Outline Close to the Peacock: Go to the menu bar and tap the outline icon but make sure you already clicked 'All items' in the Sequence View. Choose your favorite distance for the peacock but we will use 0.15" for this design.

Again, apart from the distance, watch out for the parameters to create multiple echo stitches round the embroidery design. An outline will pop up after a few seconds but feel free to change its color so that you can easily view it. How can I do this? Go back to the Sequence View, right-click the outline and select your favorite color from the dialog box that pops up.

Step 5. Edit Outline: Watch the design closely to see the jump stitches close to the peacock's neck. These stitches make the outline appear outside but you can manually tilt the outline a bit.

To do this, go back to the Sequence View, click the Shape icon on the Edit toolbar to display an array of points. Use these points to define the outlook of your outline. Move the points around to change the look of your outline. Feel free to add stippling and block once you sort out the outline.

Step 6. Stippling: Add a square or a rectangle that suits the dimension of your block. We will use a rectangle for this project. Go to the Creation toolbar, click Custom Shapes icon, and select Rectangle. Place your cursor to the exact location you want to drop the rectangle, press down the left button of your mouse, draw down the cursor right to enlarge the rectangle to the size you want, and release the mouse once you get the right size.

Check to see if the rectangle was attached to the bottom of the thread sequence. Yes, but does it tally with the color of the stippling? Perfect. The rectangle should share the color of the stippling. Go to the Properties section to select the rectangle and the Transform tab. No worries if you can't find the section on your FTC-U program. Use Toolbars instead. Deselect 'Maintain aspect ratio' because you need to use the block that works perfectly for your project.

Click Apply as soon as you get the right measurement for your rectangle.

Step 7. Combine Rectangle and Outline: Hold down the CTRL key while you select your rectangle and outline sequence. Use the left button on your mouse to select items on each sequence. Select two sequences, right-click to open a dialog box, and choose Combine. Also, locate the Transform toolbar on the screen and tap the Paper clip icon to create the Combine effect. Again, as soon as you tap Combine, open the Stitch Effects toolbar and click the Stipple icon to fill the part of the peacock close to the rectangle.

Feel free to change the stitch length or density of the stippling to suit your design. To do this, you have to right-click Properties and choose Auto Stipple sequence. Don't be in a hurry to finish this step. Mark 'Automatic Close' to avoid loose ends.

Still, feel free to use all the fills you see in the Stitch Effects toolbar to close the space between your peacock and rectangle. You can use the fancy fills but try to alternate the stitch density to create a striking effect.

Step 8. Finalizing the Block: Check if you still have the rectangle you attached in Step 6. It won't be there again. However, if your quilt block was to come with a batting tack down stitch, a placement stitch, or a fabric tack down stitch, you'll need to add a few rectangles to the design.

- Placement Stitch: Remember we created a rectangle earlier. Good. The rectangle acts as the placement stitch and it shows where the batting will be connected. Use the 8" by 11" block dimension in this project to create your placement stitch.

- Batting Tack Down Stitch: Draw another rectangle but make sure it is smaller than the previous one. You can make its width and height dimension 7.9" by 10.9". The second rectangle serves as the batting tack down stitch

- Fabric Tack Down Stitch: Copy the 8" by 11" rectangle. Paste the rectangle shape into the Sequence

Step 9. Sewing Order: See the three rectangles under the Sequence View. Take the rectangles above the Sequence View. How can I do this? Just right-click the rectangles, select Move to open a menu and click on Next. Feel free to sew rectangles above the Sequence View. Get back to the bottom of the Sequence View, click the stippling sequence, right-click to pop up a dialog box, select Cut. Top-scroll to click the 4th thing in the Sequence View, right-click to open a dialog box, click Paste. Next, sew the stippling once the rectangles have been sewn.

Step 10. Alignment: Center the stippling and rectangles vertically and horizontally. Remember that the three triangles represent your artwork. Multiselect the triangles and press the 'Run Stitch' icon to create great stitch effects.

Give the design a name before you save it. Again, use the technique to create amazing quilt blocks and your favorite embroidery designs. Stipple the design to make it appealing and charming.

Chapter Summary

- Echoing or stippling is a filler technique used in filling but you have to steady your hands to do it properly.

- Proper positioning of quilts is a good way to master echoing and stippling.

- Exercise more control on free-motion quilting by using the free-motion echo quilting foot.

In the next chapter you will learn how to make a baby quilt. See you there!

Chapter Four:
How to Make a Baby Quilt

Baby quilt! That charming, beautiful, and adorable artwork is the perfect gift for every child. It is totally different from any of those regular quilts you see. Baby quilts are cute, attractive, and they come in varieties—for boys and girls. A baby quilt is a joy to behold and one you don't get tired designing. There are unisex baby quilts, as well as those meant for boys or girls, and they all look great. Baby quilts are easy to design and you can create them in your home. In this chapter, you will learn how to make your own baby quilt and you'll see a few examples of amazing baby quilt patterns. So, get these materials handy as we run through the process of creating an adorable baby quilt.

Required Materials

- Fabrics

- Thread

- A pair of scissors

- Chalk marker

- Safety Pins

- Quilting machine

Instructions

Follow these simple steps to design your own baby quilt.

Step 1. Prepare the quilt sandwich. I have already told you how to go about it.

Step 2. Hold the quilt sandwich firmly with safety pins and draw a few designs on it with the chalk marker.

Step 3. Machines quilt the edges of your quilt and overlap the quilting needle on the design.

Congratulations! You just completed your first intermediate project.

How to Make a Green Pasture Baby Quilt

Here is an adorable baby quilt pattern with lots of beautiful images of farm animals. It is a fun, lovely, and perfect quilt every baby deserves, and you can design it with little or no assistance. Just go through the tips on how to do it here and get started with your own green pasture baby quilt.

Required Materials

- 36" white fabric

- 5/8 yard light-blue fabric

- 18" green fabric

- Few scraps of appliqué fabrics

- 27" fusible web

- 1 1/4 yard backing

- Coordinating threads (to join appliqué shapes)

- 44" by 44" batting

- Safety pins

- 4 1/2"Accuquilt square

- Fabric cutting machine

- Sowing machine

Instructions

Follow these simple steps to design a green pasture baby quilt.

Step 1. Cut 8 two-and-half inches strips; 6 four-and-half inches squares; 5 two-and-half inches squares; 12 two inches square triangles; and 4 sheep bodies backing from the white fabric. Cut the light-blue fabric to 34 1/2" × 18 1/2" rectangle.

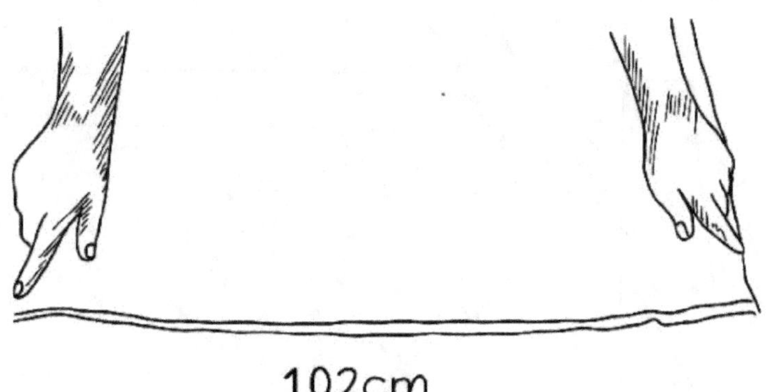

Cut 1 thirty-four-and-half inches by two-and-half inches rectangle; 10 two-and-half inches square; and 12 two inches half square triangles from the green fabric. Cut 8 sheep legs; 4 pairs of sheep ears and heads; 2 sheep bodies; 2 sheep reverse bodies; 6 sun rays' sheep ears; and 1 two-and-half circle for sun.

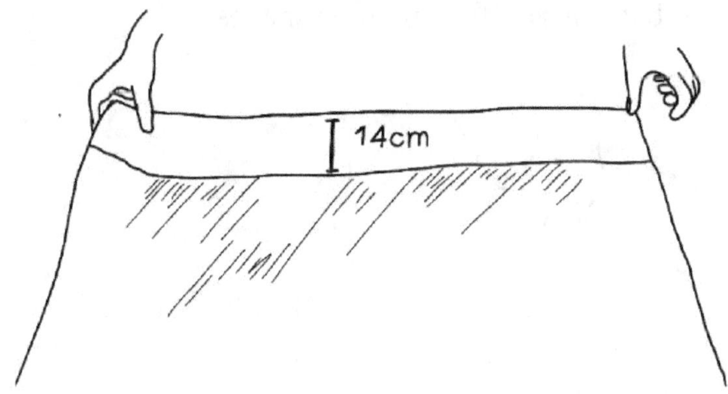

Step 2. Pin 5 sets of white and green fabric, as well as the two-and-half green squares, and sew them. Pin and sew the white half-square triangles and the 12 green fabric layers. Pin the white half-square triangles and green in pairs and sew them.

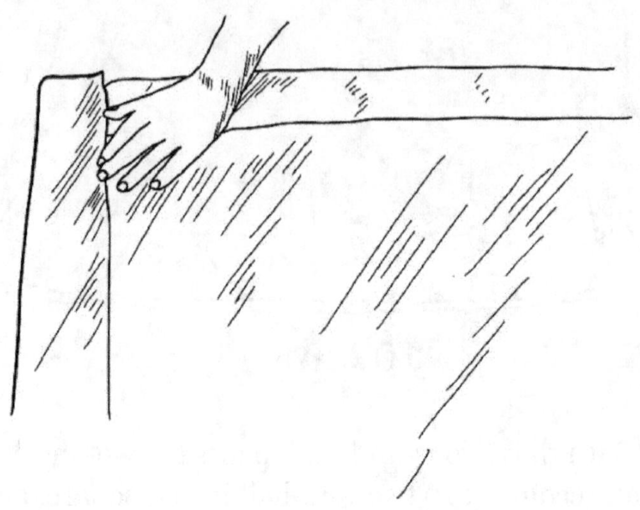

Step 3. Do border fence layout and join the units to finish the border. Join the green rectangle with the light-blue rectangle on a long edge. Pin the fence border to the base of the green rectangle, and get paper backings off the appliqué shapes.

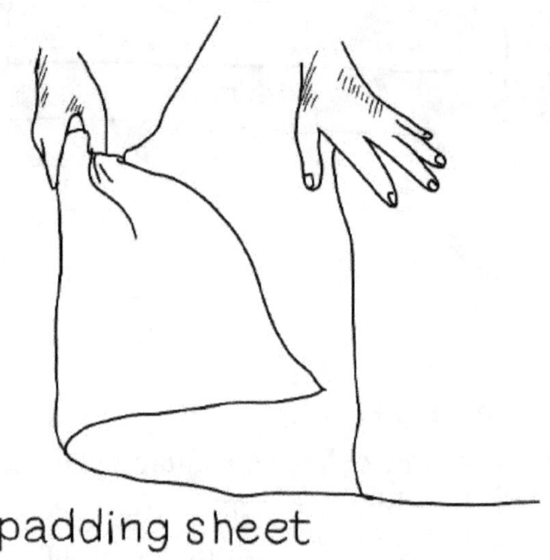

Step 4. Carefully structure clouds, sun, sheep, and sun rays. Fuse in line with manufacturer's instructions.

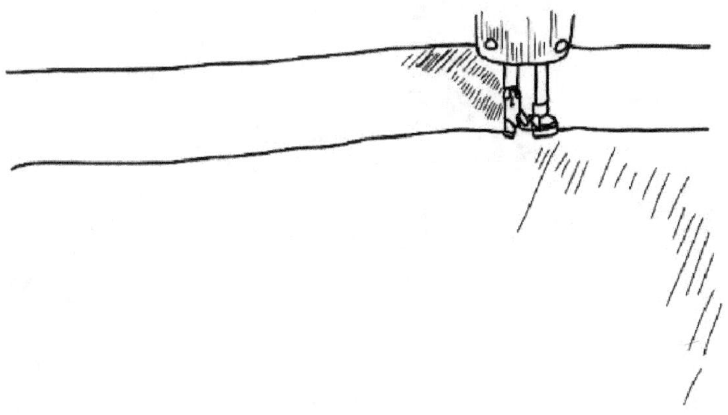

Step 5. Use a machine to appliqué design the edges but only with matching threads such as narrow satin stitch, matching thread, or narrow zigzag. Add two-and-half white borders to the sides, top, and bottom of the design.

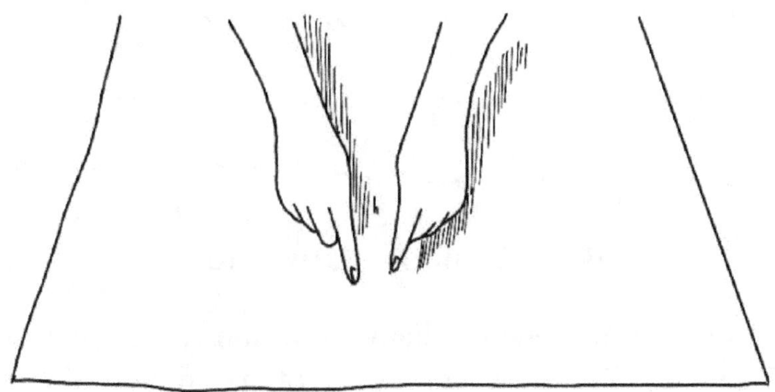

Step 6. Baste backing with quilt top, machine quilt the design, and add binding.

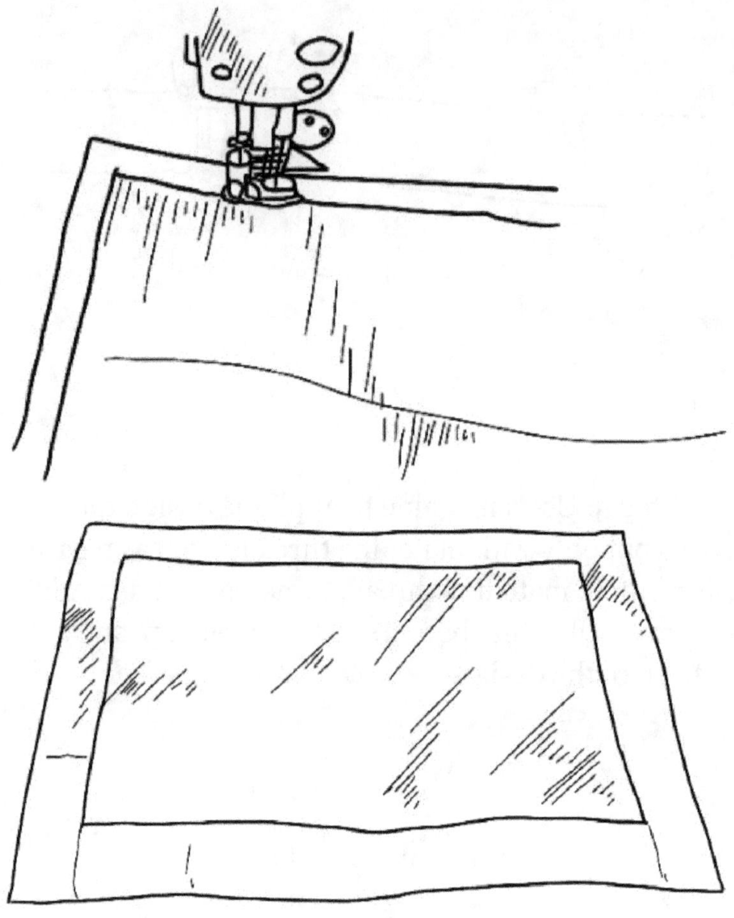

How to Make a Rainbow Baby Quilt Pattern

Call it the end of all baby quilts and you may be right. Just like the radiant colors of the rainbow, this baby quilt pattern is beautiful and appealing to the eyes. It is one pattern you don't get tired of designing.

With a bit of creativity, some scraps, or small cuts of fabric, you can design the quilt at the comfort of your home. Here's how to design the pattern.

Required Materials

- Rainbow-colored fabric

- Contrasting-colored fabric (white with red is perfect)

- 36" yard backing fabric

- 1 yard batting

- Fabric for binding (preferably white)

- A pair of scissors

- Thread

- Sewing machine

Instructions

Follow these simple steps to design your rainbow baby quilt pattern.

Step 1. Cut all layers of fabric to 6 1/2" × 28× 1/2" strips.

Step 2. Pick the white square and lay it side-down close to the right edge of your colored strip.

Step 3. Thread and needle your machine.

Step 4. Make a straight line from one corner edge to the other and sew accordingly but make sure you sew on the line.

Step 5. Join the white strip but make sure the entire stripes is not more than 30 inches.

Step 6. Repeat the process until you finish sewing the colored strips and attach them to look like a rainbow.

Step 7. Add the batting and trim excess fabric or thread.

Step 8. Do the binding with a 2" white strip.

How to Make a Charm Pack Baby Quilt Pattern

If you are looking for a simple, bright, colorful, and charming baby quilt pattern, end your search straight away. This unisex baby quilt balances tropical colors with novelty prints and its sewing process is super fast. Not only is this charming quilt a perfect gift item for every child, it is very simple to design. With a few tips, you can design a charm pack baby quilt pattern at the comfort of your home. No worries. Here is how to design it.

Required Materials

- Twenty 5" square colored fabric (preferably Club Havana)

- Twenty 5" square white fabric (Riley white is good)

- Forty 5" square white fabric

- 12" binding fabric

- 48" backing fabric

- A sewing machine

- Baby-sized quilt batting

- A pair of scissors

Instructions

Follow these simple steps to design your charm pack baby quilt pattern.

Step 1. Cut the colored fabric to 5" squares and white fabric to 5" × 36 strips.

Step 2. Needle and thread the sewing machine.

Step 3. Lay each white square on a colored square and sew 1/4" from the right side downward.

Step 4. Join a colored square to the remaining side of the white square and sew 1/4" from right downward.

Step 5. Place white strips on colored ones and sew from the bottom edge, leaving out 1/4" seam. Repeat the process until you sewn 8 rows to design the quilt top.

Step 6. Pin your quilt batting and backing in the middle of the quilt top to make a sandwich.

Step 7. Use a diamond pattern to draw diagonal lines 3 inches apart from the top of the quilt downward.

Step 8. Trim excess fabric or thread and add the quilt binding.

How to Create a Patchwork Baby Quilt

The patchwork baby quilt is an appealing and adorable design for the kid you love. Its well-laid pattern and colorful designs make it the go-to baby quilt, and words alone cannot express its uniqueness. Still, this quit is easy to design and you can create it right there in your home. Just a few tips stand between you and this baby quilt. No worries. Here is all you need to create the patchwork baby quilt.

Required Materials

- 42" by 42" batting

- 81 packaged 5" by 5" squares

- 45" fabric for backing

- Safety pins

- 12" fabric for binding

- Sewing machine

Instructions

Follow these simple steps to create your own patchwork baby quilt

Step 1. Spread out the packaged squares. Let 9 stay down while 9 lie across. Also, arrange the colors properly to print an appealing pattern. But, should the color or fabric placement raise concerns, use color to divide squares to two parts.

Step 2. Assign 1 to 9 numbers to the rows and stack the 5" by 5" squares carefully into them. Push the far-left square up but sit other squares right in the base of the pile, even as you migrate to the right.

Step 3. Move the 9 stacks of squares carefully to the sewing machine. Start sewing from the first row. Move gradually to the top square while the second square sits face-down on the top square. Use safety pins to join their right sides.

Step 4. Remove the pins as you sew the edge. Leave 1/4" space for seam allowance. But try to measure the printed edges of the packaged squares to know if the edge is up to the required 5 inches. Do the measurement before you start sewing the fabric. Feel free to use the valley or any edge you want to make your patchwork baby quilt. Still, if you are dealing with complex patterns, you will need to watch out for the correct edge.

Again, make sure that your seam allowance is consistent. The standard seam allowance for all quilt designs is 1/4". Always stick to this standard if you don't want to mess up your design.

Step 5. Make square 3 face square 2 and pin them together. Sew them 1/4" off the edge as you remove the pins.

Step 6. Continue sewing to add the other 6 blocks to the rows' right side. Start the process all over again to perfect all the 9 rows.

Step 7. Arrange your seams to one side without opening them. Seams should be pressed to one side when you are making a quilt so that they don't split open. Pressing these seams could be tasky but it is what you have to do to create neat and beautiful quilts.

Press the seams to your left if your rows have odd numbers. But, should you have even-numbered rows, press your seams to the right. With this, you can sew and join rows quickly and easily too. Again, turn over the seams and press them from up downward to keep them flat and nice.

Step 8. Sew the rows, make row 1 and 2 face each other, match the seams, and butt up the pressed seams, one against the other. Sew everything together and leave 1/4"space for seam allowance.

Don't sew the rows, one after the other, in a big section because it could mess up your work. Instead, pair the rows and sew them. Freely use pairs such as 1 &2, 3 &4, 5 & 6 until the numbers of your rows terminate. Sew the pairs to create a section of rows of two halves. Sew the halves to have a whole. With this method, you can easily manage your work and create great quilts in no distant time. Also, since the row seams will be in one direction, pressing becomes so easy. You only need to press the seams from the front to keep them flat and open.

How to Finish Your Patchwork Baby Quilt

You're done with the quilt top. Great work so far! What's next? Add your backing and batting layers first, baste them, and feel the beauty of your baby quilt. How can I choose the right batting for my quilt?

Factors to Consider Before You Choose Batting for a Quilt

Loft and fiber are two major factors you need to consider before you choose your batting.

1. Loft: How thin or which is the batting? You could have a low loft and high loft batting. Low loft means thin while high loft symbolizes thick. Low loft batting is less bulky but perfect for thinner quilts. It works fine with a running

stitch either by hand or on home machines. So, consider using low loft batting for your do-it-yourself quilting. Use high loft batting for thicker projects.

2. Fiber: What's the batting made from? Don't use batting if you don't know its source. Polyester, Cotton or Poly Blend, and 100% Cotton are the three major types of quilt batting. Each of these batting types has its merits and demerits. Recently, Bamboo, Silk, and Wool, being natural batting options, flood the market. These natural batting options come with wonderful qualities but they are very expensive.

    - Polyester: Polyester is durable and less expensive. It has amazing low loft options for hand-quilting.Its high loft options can make your quilting unique and it is good for anyone who wants to design thicker quilts.Polyester comes with warmer batting options and it provides insulation without extra weight. However, polyester shifts a lot even when quilting is not dense. In other words, polyester fibers often leave the fabric for the exterior part of the quilt.

    - Cotton: Cotton is a thick, light, and natural fiber. Its heavy weight makes it a perfect for machine quilting. Cotton washes easily and it doesn't pill. The 100% cotton shrinks slightly when quilting with it but this could be good or bad for you, depending on your quilting goal. After the first wash, I love to see my batting shrink. Why? It gives the quilt a vintage appearance and also softens it.

- Cotton Blend: Cotton blend is made up of 80 percent cotton and 20 percent polyester. It is a cotton lookalike and it rarely shrinks although it is less expensive. Cotton blend works fine with machine quilting and it is what many intermediate quilters use.

- Wool: Wool is one hundred percent natural fiber but it shrinks a lot. Don't jump at it unless you get some assurances that it will work fine for your project. Pay keen attention to the label to know whether it is pre-shrunk or not. Wool tends to resist folding and creasing but it works fine with fancy stitching and quilting. Again, wool makes hand-quilting a whole lot of fun. Wool batting is lighter-weight and warmer but very expensive. Again, wool could trigger allergic reactions in certain individuals.

- Bamboo: Bamboo is eco-friendly and a natural fiber. It aids breath ability since it is blended with Cotton. Quilts made with Bamboo batting usually come with amazing texture. Bamboo batting works fine with machine-quilted quilts.

- Fusible Batting: Fusible batting has fusible resin on its two sides. With this resin in place, you don't have to stress yourself to baste your quilt. Just iron the three layers at once if you want to baste the quilt. Sure, being a temporary fusing method, you can trust fusible batting when you are working on small scale quilts.

Be sure that the four sides of your quilt backing is bigger than your design. Press your quilt backing, spread it face-down on a surface, center your batting on it, and lower your quilt top face-up on it. Still, don't baste until you are able to see the three layers clearly from the top. Remember quilting starts from the top of your quilt. So, feel free to slightly shift the backing and batting as you deem fit.

Chapter Summary

- Baby quilts are charming, beautiful, and adorable artworks every child would like.

- The rainbow baby quilt has the radiant colors of a rainbow but you need a bit of creativity to design it.

You just designed a few colorful baby quilts. Great. In the next chapter, you will learn how to design paisley on a quilt.

Chapter Five:
Paisley on Quilt

Paisley looks charming and attractive on every quilt but very difficult to design. Still, paisley on quilt is one design you'll love to create right there in your home. Here is a fun project of a quilt designed with paisley. No worries, I will explain the process step-by-step so that you can start it straight away.

Required Materials

- An existing quilt (be it a baby quilt or a full-size quilt) or simple create a new one.

- Threads (based on your fabric)

- Needle (based on your thread)

- Gloves

- Quilting machine

Instructions

Follow these simple steps to design your own paisley on quilt project.

Step 1. Thread and needle your machine. Feel free to sketch the pattern of the quilt you want to design with chalk.

Step 2. Place your quilt below the needle and begin quilting.

Step 3. Sketch out the boundaries, secure the stitches, and create the design.

Step 4. Rotate the machine to make the needle run through your quilt. Make sure the quilt can move freely.

Step 5. Keep quilting to complete the design and secure your stitches.

Step 6. Double-stitch the edge of the quilt and trim excess fabric or thread.

How to Create a Pleasing Paisley on Quilt Pattern

Here is a beautiful paisley on quilt pattern that you can quilt with a machine or hand. Just make sure you complete the piercing and appliqué before you quilt the highly decorative paisley on quilt pattern. Here is how to design it.

Required Materials

- 36" mottled white

- 9" green print

- 36" mottled gold

- 7/8 yard teal print

- 9" gold print

- 51" square batting

- Monofilament thread (clear)

- 76" backing fabric

- Fusible web (lightweight)

- Scraps of pink and light teal print

Instructions

Follow these simple steps to design a paisley quilt pattern.

Step 1. Download your favorite paisley on quilt patterns online.

Step 2. Spread a fusible web over your pattern, paper side up. Trace the lines of each pattern with a pencil, leave 1/2" between the tracings, and cut out the fusible-web shapes, 1/4" away from traced lines.

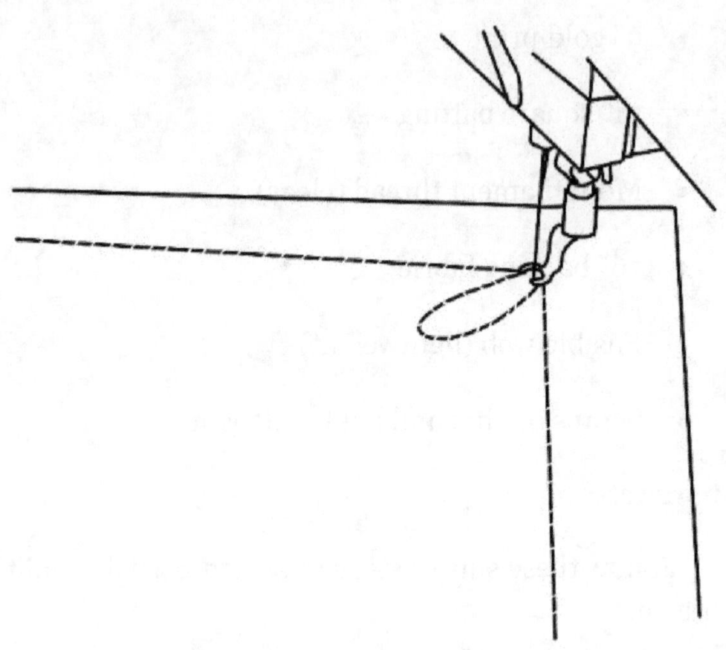

Step 3. Press fusible-web shapes on designated fabrics but follow the manufacturer's instructions. Let it cool down before you knit cut-out fabric shapes on drawn lines, or trim paper backings.

Cut 1" by 31" square from the mottled white for the center of the quilt. From the green print, cut four 2" by 33" strips for the inner border, three 2" by 31" inner border strips, and 13 Pattern D. Use the mottled gold to cut three 2" by 2" middle border strips and four 2" by 33" middle border strips.

Cut four 5" by 42" binding strips, five 1" by 4" diagonal squares, 9 Pattern A, and three 2" by 8" diagonal triangles from the teal print. Also, from the gold print, cut 9 Pattern B, 15 Pattern C, and 9 Pattern D, even as 12 Pattern E from the light teal print.

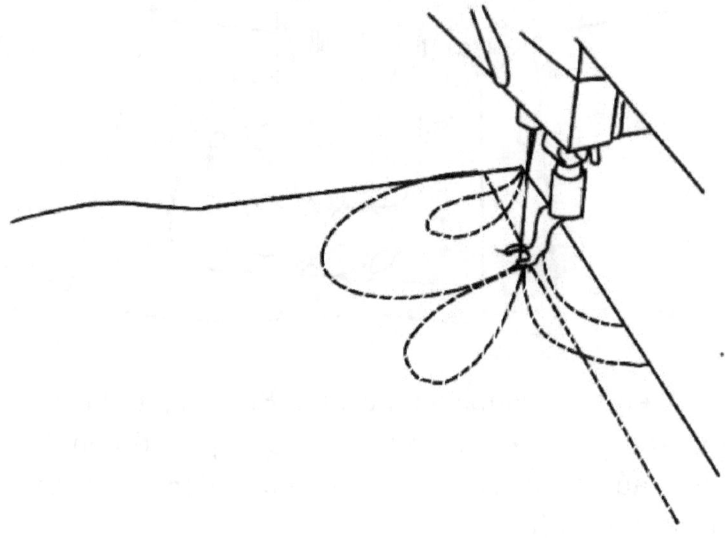

Step 4. Add inner and middle borders. Sew the opposite edges of the mottled white on the green print inner border strips, join the long green border strips to the edges, and press the seams towards the border.

Attach the middle mottled gold strips to the quilt edges before you join the long mottled gold strips to the remaining edges, and press the seams towards the border.

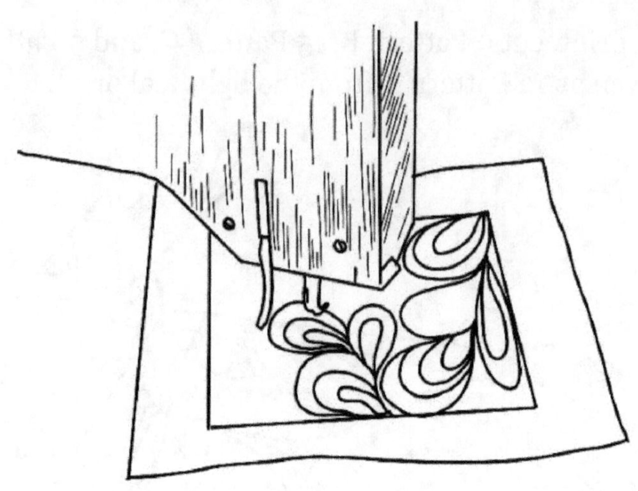

Step 5. Appliqué quilt center. Spread out the A-E appliqué pieces on the center of your quilt. Stitch the appliqué zigzag, using the clear monofilament thread on your machine.

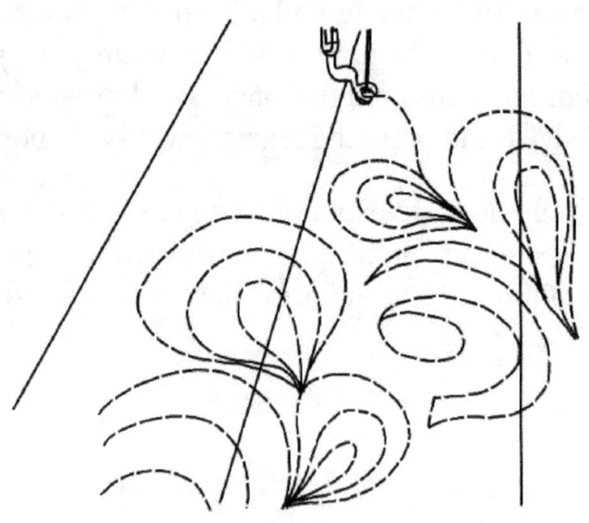

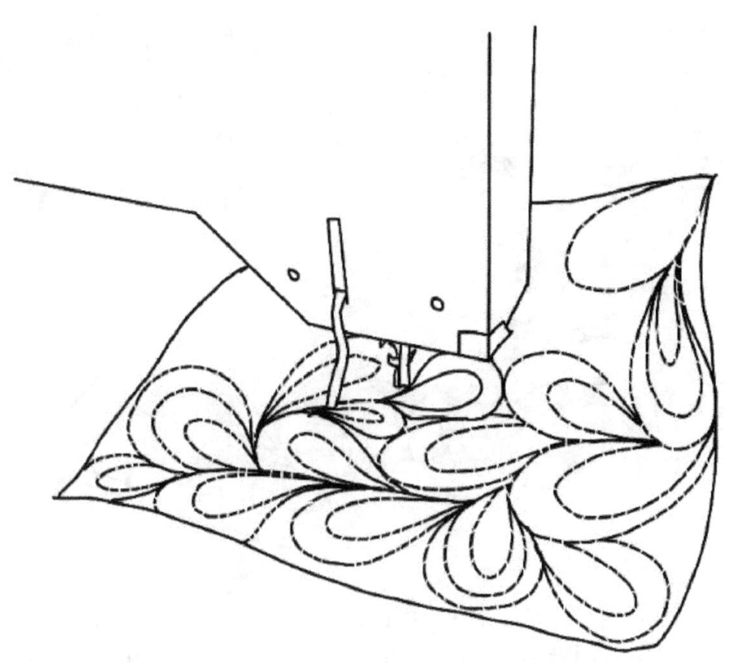

Step 6. Join the outer border. Arrange and sew
the mottled gold triangles and both small and large
teal print triangles, leaving 1/4" seam allowance. Press
the seam to the triangle and add other large triangles,
following the same process. Sew opposite exterior
center edges together and press seams towards the
center border.

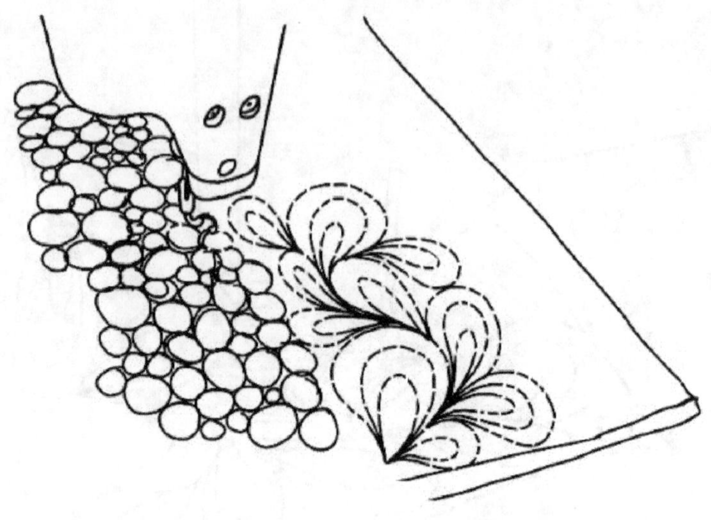

Step 7. Finish the quilt. Baste the batting, backing, and quilt top, and bind the quilt with the teal print binding strips.

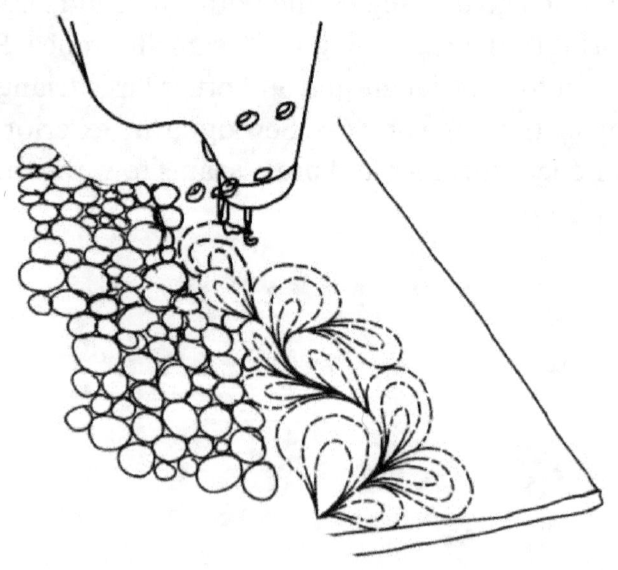

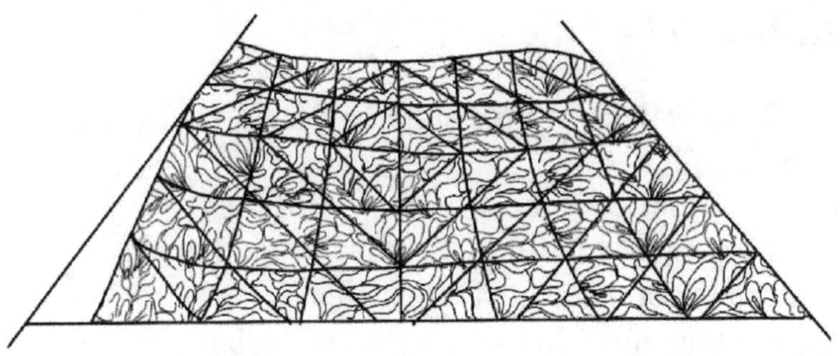

How to Design a Cotton Quilt

Here is a unique homemade quilt you can present as a gift for everyone. Again, it is a lovely quilt for babies. Sewing a Cotton quilt at the comfort of your home is personally gratifying. Use your favorite fabric and pattern to design a unique cotton quilt. Here is how to design the quilt.

Required Materials

- 46" × 54" fabric (100% cotton)

- 46" × 56" backing (100% cotton)

- 90" × 54" batting (100% cotton)

- A pair of scissors

- Bodkin

- Yarn

- Tape Measure

Instructions

Follow these simple steps to design your own cotton quilt

Step 1. Spread out the right sides of backing materials opposite each other on a surface and add the backing on either side of the materials.

Step 2. Pin all edges evenly to tack the three layers.

Step 3. Serge exterior edges of the four sides, leaving a 6" by 8" gap at the starting point, and drawing the quilt out through the gap.

Step 4. Hand-sew the gap to seal the quilt and iron the quilt to prepare it for tufting.

Step 5. Cut yarn 6 inches long, measure rug, and sew tufts 12" apart. Thread bodkin, pull it through, and tie the knot.

You just designed your own cotton quilt, congratulations.

How to Design Paisley Shorts

Sewing novices and intermediate quilters tend to find paisley shots intimidating to design. Some say that the processes are hectic while others simply believe that such projects aren't just for them. Well, with a little work and patience, you can surely design a pair of nice and comfortable elastic paisley shots at the comfort of your home. No worries. I will run you through the process of designing beautiful shots for men and women.

Paisley Shots for Women

Follow these simple steps to design a woman's paisley shot.

Step 1. Sketch your pattern: Create your pattern from the scratch or trace an outline on a piece of drawing or craft paper to save time. Here's how to trace a pair of shots.

- Fold the shorts in half but ensure that front pockets stay outside while you trace the outline on a craft paper.

- Create 1 inch seam allowance at the sides and bottom of the pattern.

- Create 4 cm space for the waistband at the top of the pattern and use scissors to cut out the pattern.

Step 2. Pin the pattern to your fabric: Fold the fabric in half, spread the pattern on it, and pin both together. Just make sure that the center part of the pattern rests directly on the fabric's folded edge. Still, to get the whole thing done accurately, sketch the pattern on your fabric before you cut it.

Step 3. Cut the fabric: Carefully cut the fabric along the outline with sharp sewing shears to get the shots' one full side. Repeat the process to create the second full side of your shots. Lay the two pieces on a surface but ensure that the right sides face each other. Pin each piece along the rounded seams and remember that you'll still stitch the seams to align the shorts.

Step 4. Stitch the seams: Machine-sew the shorts along the seams. Use a backstitch if you want to hand-stitch the shorts. Still, leave 1" seam allowance, and you'll be left with what looks like a tube of fabric.

Step 5. Turn out the shorts: Flip out the shorts to properly sit the center back and front of the fabric. Sewn seams occupy the outside edges once you join the two pieces together. Rotate the shots to align the seams evenly and down to the center. Sewn seams will form the shorts' crotch once you complete sewing.

Step 6. Sew inner thigh seams: Flatten the fabric, pin both sides, and sew along the seams to complete each leg of the shots. Keep the 1 inch seam allowance and use a zigzag stitch to sew all the sides together. Still, make sure that the seams fall on the inner thigh.

Step 7. Create a waistband: Turn over the upper edge of your fabric to accommodate the elastic band. Pin and stitch the waistband along the edge of your fabric. Here's how to create the waistband.

- Fold the top-part of your fabric by 2" to provide space for your waistband elastic.

- Use your sewing machine to sew a straight stitch along the edge of your fabric. Feel free to backstitch with your hand.

- Create a small hole in the seam edge to run the waistband elastic.

Step 8. Run the elastic through your waistband: Pass the elastic through the hole in the seam edge to the other end of your waistband and sew the opening.

Just make sure that the size of the elastic is roughly 3 inches less than your waist. Why? Elastic must stretch if you want it to stay secure. The extra space can make the shorts secure and fit.

Pin one side of the elastic so that you can run it freely through the waistband. Pull out the two ends from the waistband before you zigzag-stitch the elastic to close the opening.

Step 9. Hem the shots: Fold each leg's bottom edge by 1 inch, pin it, and sew to design a hem around the leg. Here is how to do it.

- Create 1/2" seam allowance as you sew the hemmed part around the shots' leg opening.

- Sew the shorts' front and back separately, not together.

Paisley Shorts for Men

Paisley shorts for men are slightly different from those meant for women but you can master them in no distant time. Here's how to design paisley shorts for men.

Step 1. Download patterns online: Patterns for men paisley shorts are available online, free of charge. Print the pattern on A4 paper but leave the 'scale printing' box unchecked. Each pattern you download comes with some instructions. Make sure you abide by all the instructions as you try to cut out the patterns or tape them to their designated places.

Step 2. Pin the pattern on your fabric: Spread your fabric on a surface, with its wrong side facing up, and pin the pattern on it. Here's how to do it.

- Pin the pattern to the wrong side of the fabric. Sketch the pattern on the fabric with a sewing pencil or chalk to achieve accuracy.

- Check to see whether the pattern comes with seam allowance. Fold the fabric to form a double layer and pin the pattern to it.

Step 3. Cut out the fabric: Use sharp sewing shears to cut out each piece of the pattern from the fabric. Cut out the pieces again but in reverse order and pin the pieces together.

Step 4. Design and stitch the back pockets: Pin pocket pieces appropriately on the shorts, double-stitch pockets' top and sew the pockets' sides and bottom. Press pockets' edges with iron, create an edge for the pocket opening, double-stitch the edge, and sew the pockets to the fabric.

Step 5. Design and stitch the front pockets: Design the front pockets the way you created the back pockets. Here's how to do it.

- Press the edges of the pocket pieces with an iron.

- Double-stitch the pocket's top hem and create an opening for the pocket.

- Pin the pocket to the shorts and double-stitch its sides and bottom.

Step 6. Sew the crotch: Hold the shorts firm, pin its back portions, and sew the portions along the crotch. Here is how to complete the process.

- Hold the right sides, with each facing the other, and pin the pieces firmly.

- Shape each side of the seam to 9.5 mm with sharp sewing shears. Also, clip and curve the bottom part of your crotch seam.

- Sew up the crotch seam with a flat felled seam.

Step 7. Stitch the remaining parts of the seams: Stitch side seams— right and left sides— and the inseam, the seams within the shorts. Lock the inseam with the raw edge to avoid excess fraying as soon as you sew the inseam. Sew the side seams, using the flat felled seam technique.

Step 8. Hem the shorts: Fold up the bottom hem and hold it firmly by double-stitching the top of the hem. Use an iron to press the bottom hem to design a sturdy fold on the shorts.

Step 9. Sew the lining of the waistband: Hold the shorts, make the right sides of the waistband face each other, pin it, and sew the waistband lining down to the waist. Just line up the joint of the waistband evenly, like the middle of the back waist part.

Step 10. Join the elastic waistband: Create 1/2"overlap on the edges of the raw ends of the elastic waistband and zigzag-switch it. But make sure the elastic is shorter than the elastic waistband so that it can sit well on your waist. How can I do this? Just measure the wearer's waist round and subtract 3 inches from the measurement value. The elastic band can stretch out if you follow this process and the designed shorts will be nice on the person wearing it.

Step 11. Fold the elastic into the material: Spread the shorts on a surface, pin the elastic on it, and sew to finish the shorts. No worries. Just follow these simple steps.

- Lay shorts on a surface, with the back waist facing up. Pin the elastic in the middle of the waist.

- Turn the shorts, with the front waist facing up. Half-fold the band and pin it in the middle of the front waist.

- Divide the band into some evenly-spaced points and pin it on 8 or 10 different places on the fabric.

- Fold the edge of the lining on the elastic waistband but let the wrong side face out. Stretch the elastic gently a bit and sew straight along the edge.

- Flip the shorts to turn out the right sides. Stretch the elastic gently a bit before you double-stitch the top of the waistband.

Chapter Summary

- Paisley looks charming and attractive on every quilt but very difficult to design.

- A Cotton quilt is a beautiful and unique homemade quilt for every child.

- You need a bit of creativity and plenty of endurance to create adorable paisley on quilt projects.

The next chapter is dedicated for Strip-pieced contemporary chevron designs. Lots of things to learn there!

Chapter Six:
Strip-Pieced Contemporary Chevron

Strip-pieced contemporary chevron designs are unique. Not only are they beautiful and appealing, the designs are so simple that you can create them at home. Yes, in this chapter, I will teach you how to use Strip cutouts to design a quilt with contemporary chevron. Sure, you will love this fun project and you'll want to create it your own way any time soon. Also, in this chapter, you'll see other contemporary chevron projects to design. However, let us quickly run through the first project for the day— a contemporary chevron quilt.

Required Materials

- A well-feathered quilt (make sure it has adequate space you can work with)

- Fabric strips (balanced rhapsody color).

- Rotary cutter

- Scale

- Sewing machine

-

Instructions

Follow these simple steps to design your own quilt with contemporary chevron.

Step 1. Scale your fabrics and use the rotary cutter to cut the fabric strips to smaller pieces.

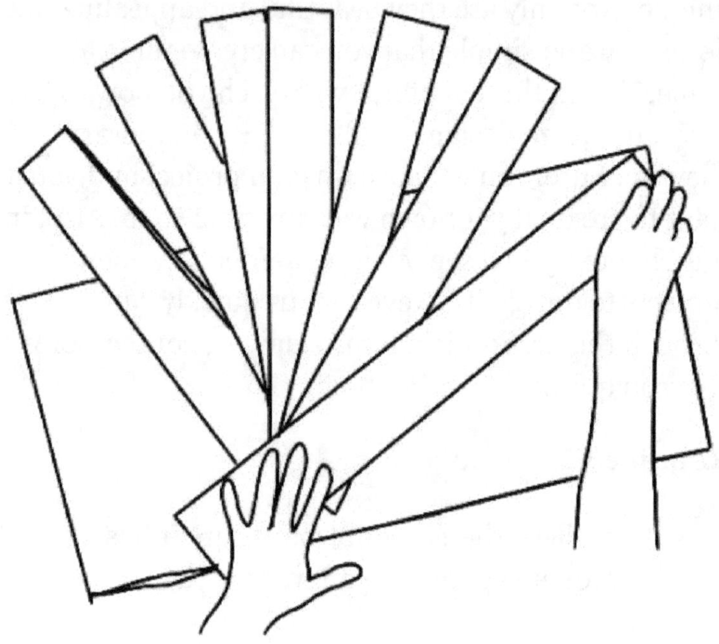

Step 2. Trim your background strips to the size of the small fabric pieces and carefully arrange the pieces. Create a few arrows that you'll work with.

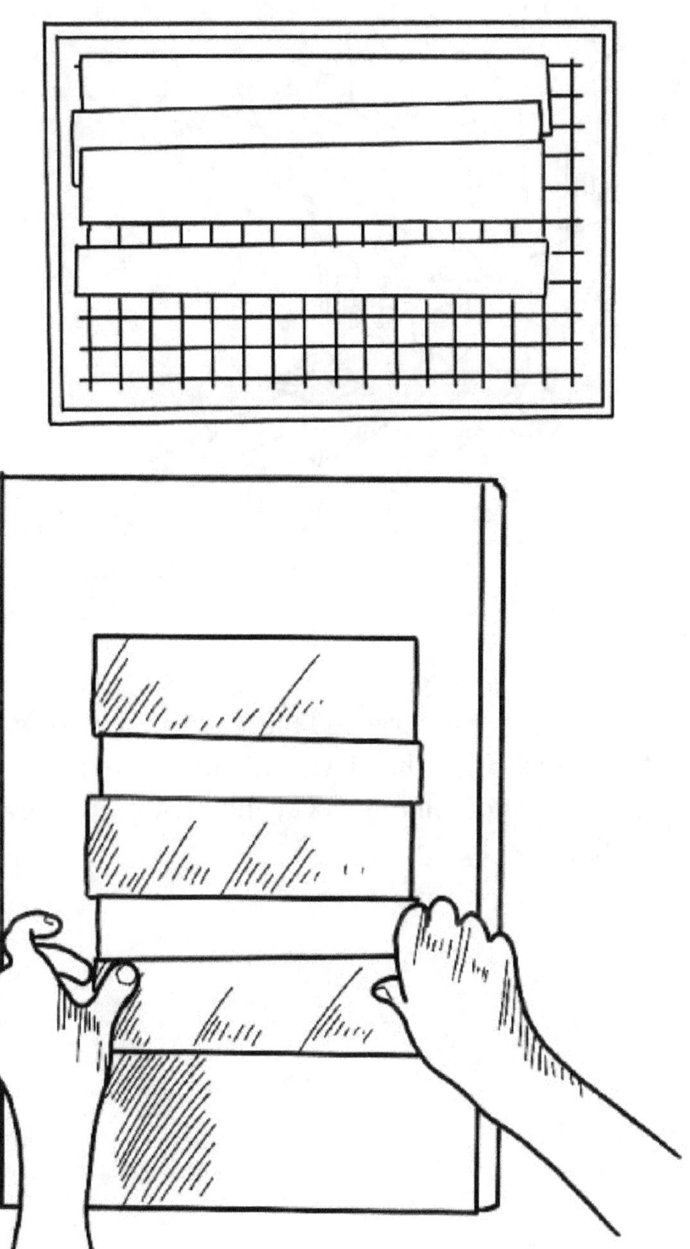

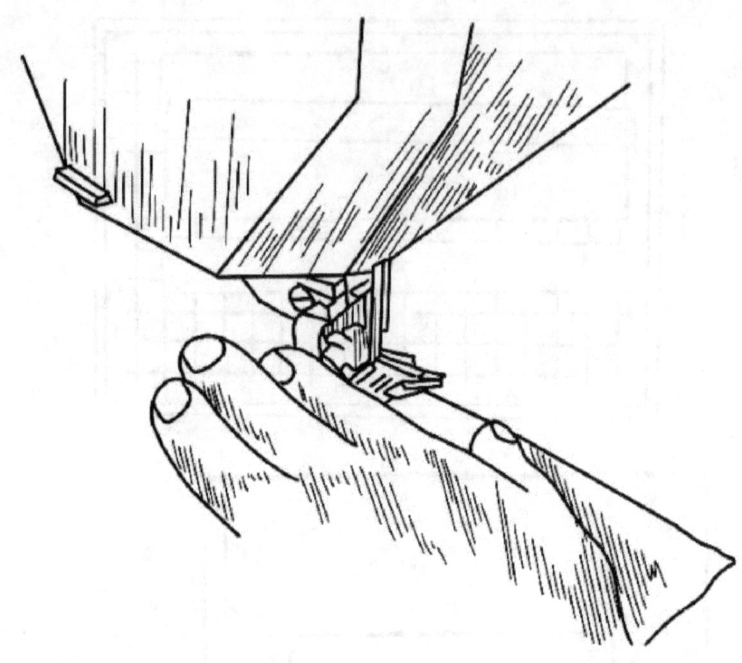

Step 3. Sew the arranged pieces together to create the first block. Heat the block with an iron to rid puckers or smoothen the block, and arrange the sewn pieces together again.

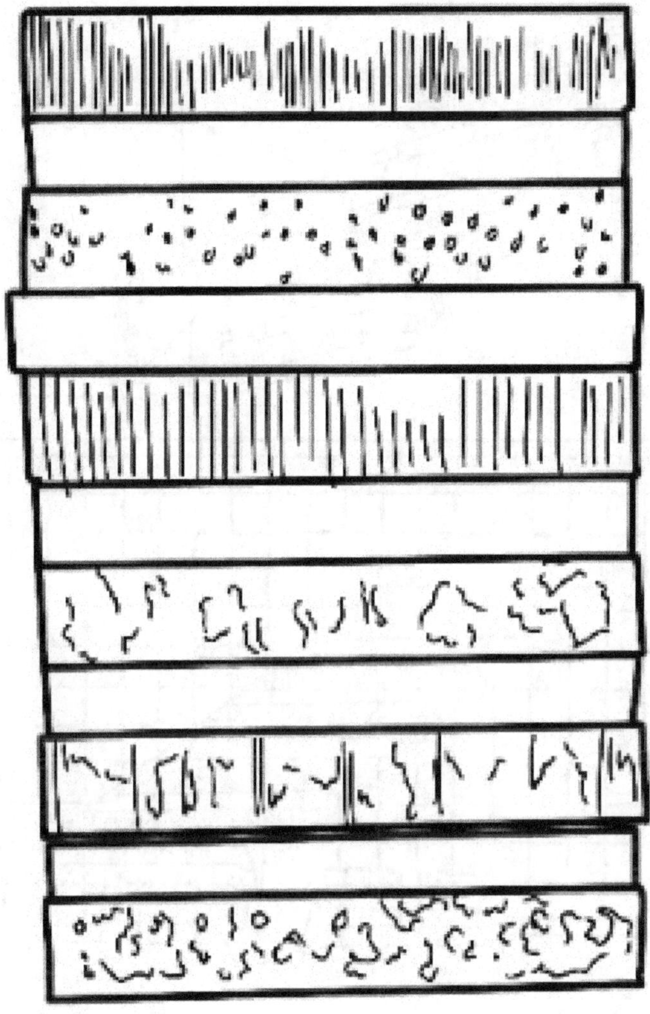

Step 4. Trim excess fabric edges until it is 45 degree. Also, trim the edges of your block to make the quilt appear neat and well-shaped.

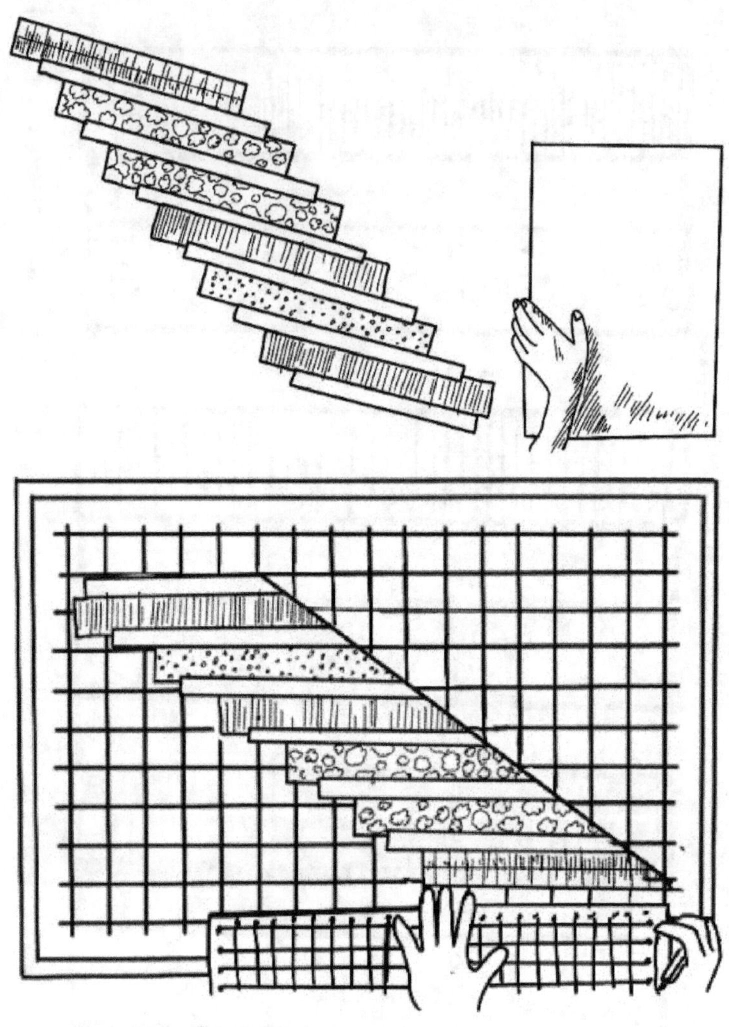

Step 5. Repeat steps 3 and 4 until you use all the pieces to create pattern blocks. Rotate the fabric but vary its directions, and design the pattern on your quilt.

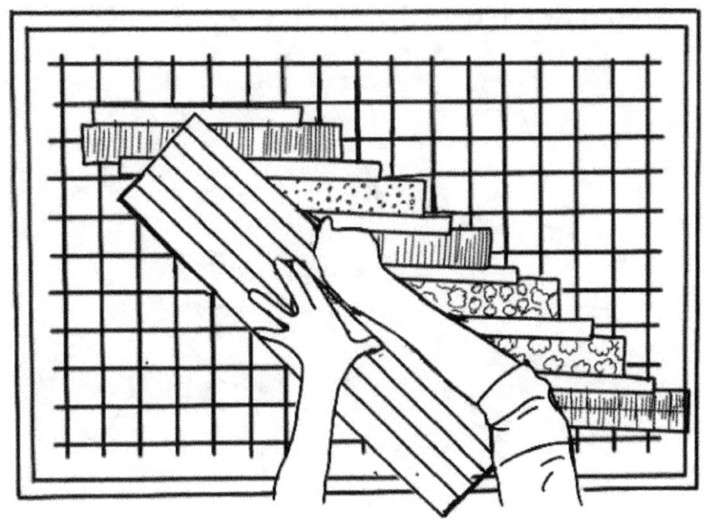

Step 6. Lay the pattern on your quilt and start quilting, one pattern before the other.

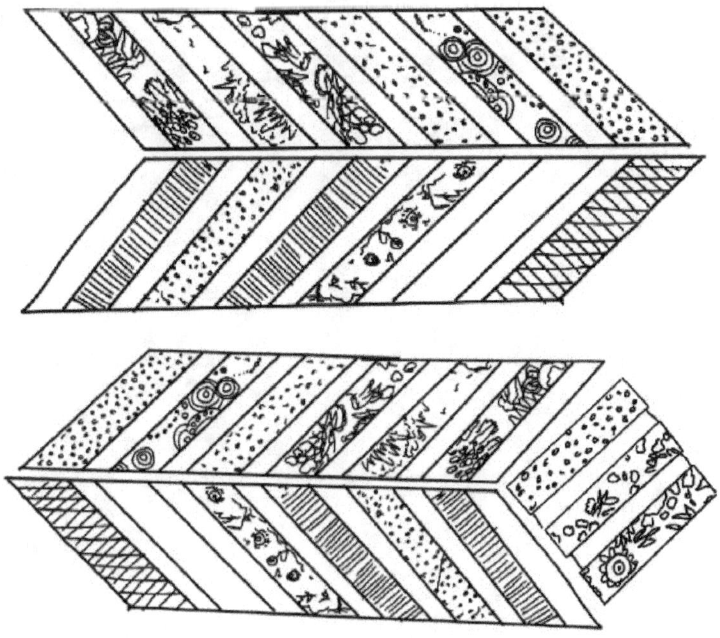

Step 7. Stitch the edges to secure the quilt.

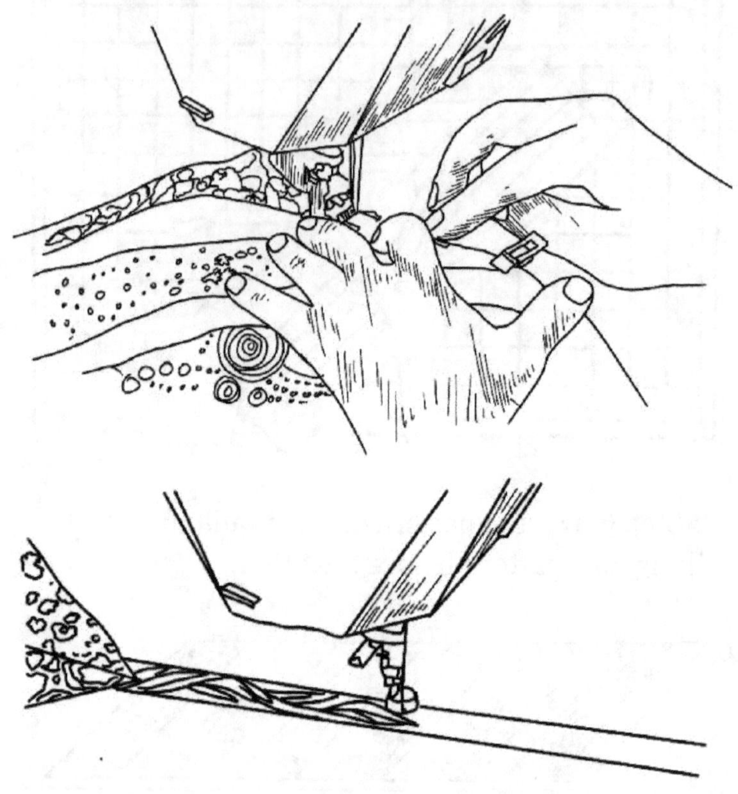

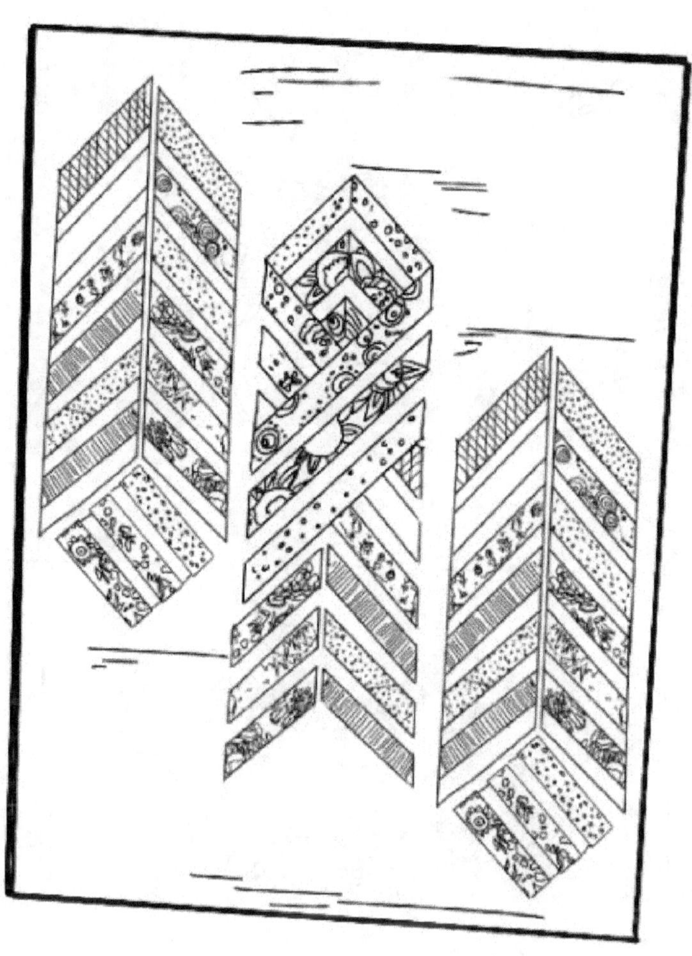

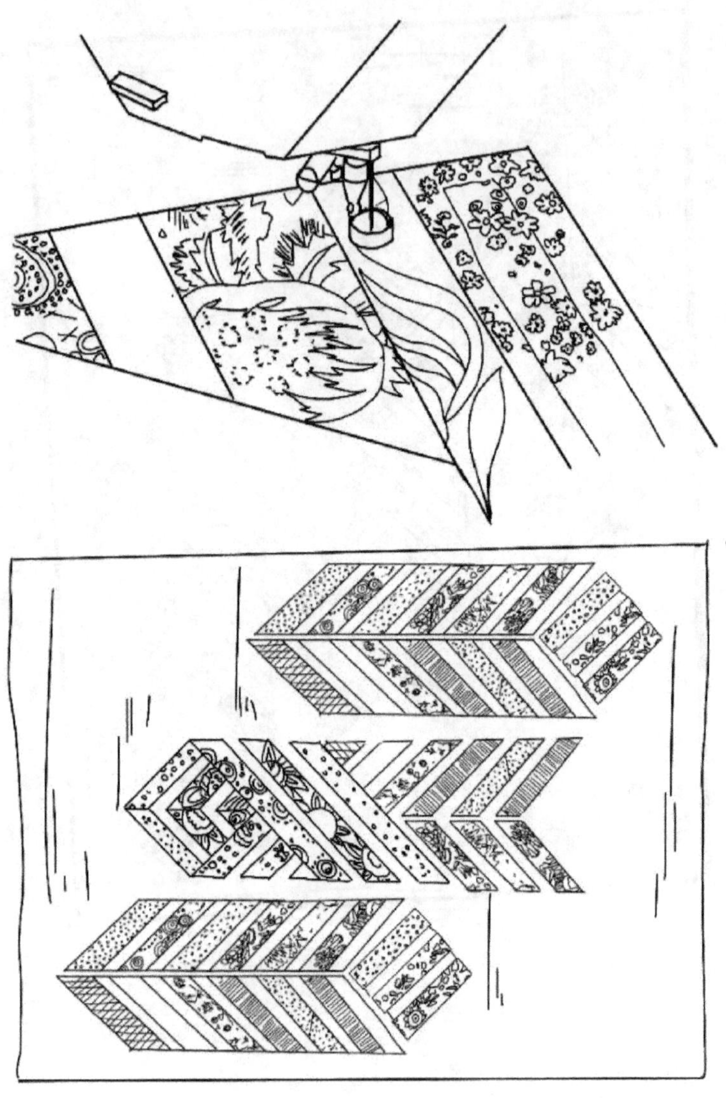

Feel free to show off your awesome project.

How to Design a Bandana Bracelet

Bracelets look good and most people, especially kids, love them. A bandana bracelet is just like other bravelets— very easy to design. Just a few tricks and you'll be on your way to design your first bandana bracelet. Here is how you can design it right there in your home.

Required Materials

- Fabric strips

- Lollipop sticks

- Hot glue

- Fish tank tubing

Instructions

Follow these simple steps to create your own bandana bracelet.

Step 1. Cut the fabric to a few 1 inch strips and remove the strings.

Step 2. Cut tubing to your size, or the size of the person you want to design it for, and cut lollipop sticks to small pieces or chunks. Put some hot glue on each side of the tube and insert the lollipop stick to form a small circle. Don't add the glue on the two ends at a time. No. It has to be one after the other.

Step 3. Add some hot glue to the hem of the fabric to gum it to the tube. Muffle the fabric all over the tube. Feel free to twist the fabric when there's need.

Step 4. Continue the process until you cover the tube with fabric completely.

A 22" bandana strip is enough to create a bracelet for a small child. But, should you run out of fabric in the process, splash a little glue on another strip, and roll it over the tube. Still, you'll need to muffle extra strips of fabric to fill up the seams.

Step 5. Trim excess fabric and add more glue to secure the bracelet.

How to Design a 5 Inch Fabric Flower

Consider spicing up your dressing with the 5 inch fabric flower. It is bold, beautiful, attractive, and charming, and it'll surely give you a unique look each time you wear a dress adorned with this lovely design. Still, you can give it out to someone who means the world to you. How can I create it? No worries. I am going to show you how you can design your own 5 inch fabric flower straight away.

Required Materials

- 23" by 3.25" fabric scrap

- A pair of scissors

- Needle and thread

- Marker

- Template

- Tiny piece of felt

Instructions

Follow these simple steps to design your own 5 inch fabric flower

Step 1. Download a template online to get started. But, if you already have one to use, fine. Place the template on the wrong side of your fabric, trace it with a marker, and sketch 9 or more petals on the fabric.

Step 2. Carefully use the scissors to cut the pattern out. Slip a thread into your normal hand needle and hem the lower edge of your fabric.

Step 3. Sew the fabric ends together to form the shape of a flower and stitch the center of the fabric to hold or secure the flower.

Step 4. Adorn the flower with a button or add other lovely embellishments.

So cute, isn't it?

How to Design a Herringbone Quilt

Herringbone quilts look appealing, beautiful, and charming, but difficult to design for some quilters. Still, you can successfully design it in your home. Just follow these simple steps to design a homemade Herringbone quilt.

Required Materials

- Quilting fabric (different colors)

- Thread

- Batting

- Ruler

- Cutting mat

- Rotary Cutter

- Sewing machine

- Safety pins

Instructions

Follow these simple steps to create your own Herringbone quilt.

Step 1. Cut the fabric to 42" by 63" blanket size. Don't forget that the quilt combines some chevrons of four squares each and each square has two triangles. Feel free to alter the squares to suit your favorite dimension. Cut 8" by 8" squares of fabric for the triangles. Fold the squares in half and cut diagonally. Repeat the process until your triangles are enough for the quilt.

Still, you can make each chevron unique and different. Just cut 8" square from each fabric, fold in half to have 4 triangles. Also, ready twenty seven 8" squares gray fabric.

Step 2. Join the fabric pieces. With right sides facing each other, sew one colored triangle with a gray one but leave 1/4" seam allowance. Press-iron the seam, clip extra fabric, and repeat the process till you have 54 squares for the quilt.

Arrange and rotate the squares till you use the colored fabric to form a 'V' shape. Fold the two squares, one on the other, but allow their right sides to face each other. Line the corners equally, sew along the edges, but don't forget to leave the 1/4" seam allowance. Iron the edges of the seam to keep it flat.

Use the same process for the remaining 2 squares. Join the top and bottom edges of the chevron. Line up the center seam before the join the pieces together, and iron the edges of the seam once you sew the pieces. Pin chevron columns to the point where the seams intersect but align columns' tip with the tip of the seams. Join all the columns and iron the seams flat. Don't drag the iron on the fabric. Instead, raise it and place it on the part you want to press. You just finished the quilt top.

Step 3. Design the quilt sandwich. Spread the backing on a surface, right side facing down, and smoothen the batting on it. Spread the quilt top on it, right side facing up, and pin everything on each triangle firmly.

Step 4. Quilt along the top of the seam till you sew the whole quilt.

Step 5. Bind the quilt. Trim excess batting and backing, but feel free to leave extra 1/4" batting if you love a fuller binding. Sew dyed colored fabric scraps to bind the quilt, muffle some along the Quilt's perimeter, and iron-press the quilt.

You have just designed a Herringbone quilt, congratulations.

How to Create a Zigzag Quilt Pattern

A zigzag quilt pattern is very unique but it requires a little bit of creativity. Visualize how you really want it to look like before you start quilting the pattern. Here is how you can design your special zig zag quilt pattern right there in your home.

Required Materials

- 5" square charms (150)

- 36" border fabric

- 18" binding fabric

- 62" by 72" batting

- 144" backing fabric

- Iron

- Sewing machine

- Safety pins

Instructions

Follow these simple steps to design your own zig zag quilt pattern

Step 1. Trim off the selvages from the border fabric. Cut out eight 4 1/2 inch strips from the fabric. Cut the square charms and batting as shown in the 'Required Materials.'

Step 2. Sew right sides of the squares together but maintain the 1/4" seam allowance. Don't forget that you are to sew the squares in rows. Use iron to press the seams on all the rows.

Step 3. Sew together rows 1 and 2; 3 and 4; 5 and 6, till you finish sewing all the 14 rows. Sew the combined rows to assemble the quilt top, and use iron to flatten the seams.

Step 4. Join the end of the border pieces until it is an 80" piece. Repeat the process to join the remaining 6 border pieces.

Step 5. Spread the quilt top on a surface, line the first border piece over the edge of the top, pin, and sew them together. Cut the lower edge of the border to make it equal with the quilt-top bottom.

Step 6. Line the second border piece over the quilt-top bottom, pin, and sew them together. Trim the border to equal it to the size of the quilt.

Step 7. Repeat the process to join other border pieces on the top and sides of the quilt. Flatten the seams again with your iron.

Step 8. Spread the backing piece, wrong side up. Lay the batting on it, and the quilt top will follow, wrong side on the batting. Baste and quilt.

Step 9. Bind the quilt with straight or bias binding.

How to Create Fabric Pumpkins

Only a look at fabric pumpkins is satisfying and fun. Should we talk about the glowing colors of the design or the multiple eyes queueing to catch a glimpse of the person using the fabric? Sure, you too can create the design. Yes, creativity is key but you will also need the tips here.

Required Materials

- Pillow stuffing

- Fabric (orange, purple, and stripe colors)

- Needle

- Thread

- A ruler

- A pair of scissors

- hot glue

- Sewing machine

- Fabric or felt (for stem and leaves)

- Basting stitch

- Twine or string

Instructions

Follow these simple steps to design your own fabric pumpkin

Step 1. Cut fabric to rectangular shapes. Vary the dimensions so that the shapes can be a little bit different from one another. Just remember that the width of a regular pumpkin is twice its height. Still, feel free to cut your fabric to many shapes so far each shape complements the other. You may cut your fabric according to this pattern.

- Orange fabric: 15.5" by 7.5" strips.

- Purple fabric: 32" by 13" strips.

- Stripe fabric: 21" by 16" strips.

Step 2. Hold the right sides of the fabric together, fold it in half, and sew with hand or machine, or put little hot glue on the side of the seam.

Step 3. Sew the lower part of the fabric pumpkin. Use your hand to sew a wide basting and join it with the pumpkin's bottom. Lift the pumpkin's bottom a bit to see if it is tightly sewn. Stitch it a few times to firmly hold or secure it.

Step 4. Turn out the right side of the fabric pumpkin, stuff it, and close its top side very well. Yet, you may need to conserve your stuffing. How? Hold the center of your stuffing and make a small hole there. Put fabric scraps or plastic bags in the hole first before you place your stuffing on it.

Step 5. Sew your basting stitch on the stuffing and seal it up, just like you closed the fabric pumpkin bottom. Close the top and stitch it a few times to firmly hold or secure the basting.

Step 6. Add finishing touches. Muffle the string or twine all over the pumpkin three or four times, or as many times as you want. Just make sure it is very tight and the tying should terminate in the fabric pumpkin's bottom. Should the bottom knot worry you, shape a felt or fabric into a circle, sprinkle little hot glue under it, and place it on the knot.

Still, feel free to add a few leaves and stems to embellish your design. Use the hot glue to attach any embellishment you want.

Herringbone Baby Quilt Pattern

Regular baby quilts look simple and beautiful, just like our quilt pattern for today, the Herringbone baby quilt. Again, this pattern blends well with most modern baby quilts. Maybe there's an expectant mum in your place and you've been wondering what to give the baby when it finally arrives, here is the Herringbone baby quilt pattern. You don't know how to create it? No worries. Here's the how.

Required Materials

- 63" fabric A

- 63" fabric B

- 63" fabric (pink elephant for quilt back)

- 13 1/2" fabric for binding

- 40" by 60" quilt batting

- Safety pins

- Rotary cutter

- Ruler

- Sewing machine

Instructions

Follow these simple steps to design your own Herringbone baby quilt pattern.

Step 1. Cut Fabric A and B to 13.75" by 13.75" (seven pieces each).

Step 2. Mark the fabric by sketching a diagonal 'X' on all the wrong sides of the fabric's lightest pieces.

Step 3. Place one marked square of fabric A on one square of Fabric B, with right sides facing each other, and pin the two together.

Step 4. Repeat the process till you pin fabric A and fabric B squares.

Step 5. Adjust the foot of your sewing machine to set seam allowance to 1/4" and stitch either side of the pinned layers of fabric.

Step 6. Evenly divide the squares to 4 parts and cut the layers with your rotary cutter to have 8 smaller pieces. Sew the edges of the pieces and trim excess pieces.

It was simple running the steps. Yes, and you just designed a Herringbone baby quilt pattern.

How to Design a Bandana Quilt

Here is a rare but beautiful quilt you can design and complete at the comfort of your home in only a few hours. A bandana quilt is a perfect gift for anyone you truly value, and it is very simple to create. All you need to do to create this quilt is follow the instructions here.

Required Materials

- Quilt batting

- Red, white, and blue bandana

- A pair of scissors

- Ruler

- Sewing machine

- Threads

- Safety pins

- A pressing iron

Instructions

Follow these simple steps to design your own bandana quilt.

Step 1. Spread the bandana to create your favorite bandana pattern.

Step 2. Arrange the bandanas, clipping their right sides together. Leave 1/4" seam allowance and sew the bandanas along their edges. Just sow everything in a row. And, later on, pick all the rows and sew them together. However, don't try to perfectly align the edges of the bandanas or match up their corners. There's no way you can have a straight bandana.

Step 3. Repeat the above processes to perfect the other side of your quilt.

Step 4. Flatten the seams by pressing them with iron.

Step 5. Spread the quilt on a surface, wrong side facing up. Lay the quilt batting on it, trim the batting to fit the quilt, but make sure that the quilt sides are at least 3 inches more than the batting. Why? Bandana or batting may shake in the process of quilting.

Step 6. Pin the quilt batting, sew a few lines to firmly hold the quilt and batting, and remove the safety pins.

Step 7. Lay the quilt on a surface, batting side facing down, and spread the second quilt on it, wrong side facing up, to design the quilt sandwich.

Step 8. Leave an opening of 10 inches where you'll flip out the right side of the quilt. Sew everything together, only on the edges.

Step 9. Trim the excess fabric on be edges and turn out the right side of the quilt.

Step 10. Hand-stitch or use a machine to sew the 10 inches' opening and flatten the edges with iron.

Step 11. Quilt a few lines to firmly hold the front and back sides of the quilt.

Here you are. You just designed a bandana quilt.

Chapter Summary

- Strip-pieced contemporary chevron designs are appealing and simple to design but you have to be creative.

- A bandana bracelet looks perfect on many people and you can vary the design as you want.

In the next chapter you will learn how to create shattered frame quilts.

Chapter Seven: Shattered Frame Quilt

Shattered frame quilts are beautiful, appealing, and easy to design. Again, you don't need lots of fabric to create one. There are lots of free patterns online that you can download to get started. To create one, you'll need to randomly stitch a few 2 1/2" strips together and trim them down a bit. No worries. In this chapter, I will teach you how to create a quilt and design it with a shattered frame. Also, you'll learn how to design some other quilts. But, before then, let's create a shattered-frame designed quilt. Here's how to design it.

Required Materials

- Fabrics (suitable for a quilt sandwich)

- Threads

- Needle (according to threads)

- Fabric scraps

- Sewing machine

- A pair of scissors

Instructions

Follow these simple steps to design your quilt with a shattered frame.

Step 1. Ready your scrap fabrics by cutting them into small strips.

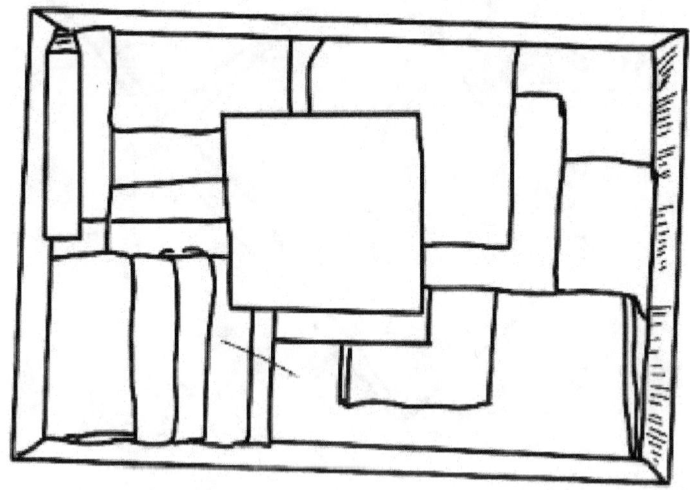

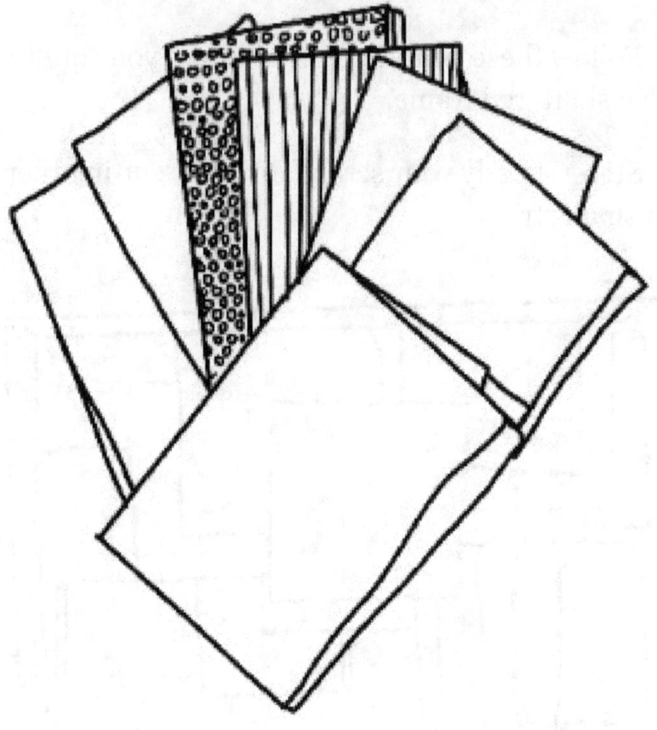

Step 2. Thread and needle your sewing machine.

Step 3. Carefully arrange the strips and stitch then from one corner to the other.

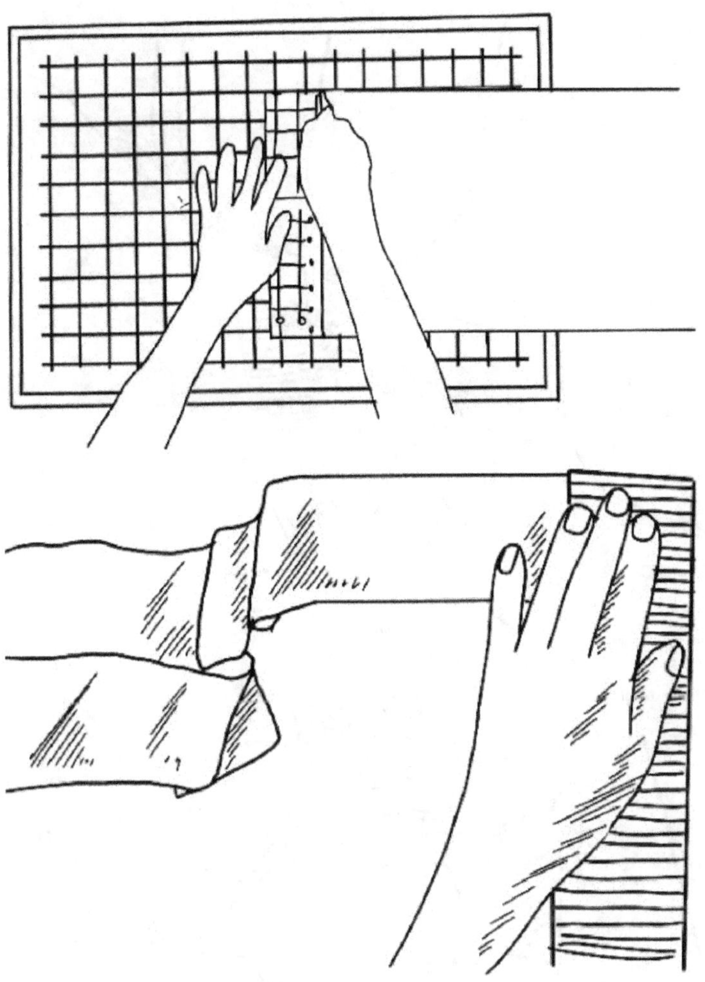

Step 4. Use the scissors to trim the edges of the strips.
Turn out the strip to join 2 strips together.

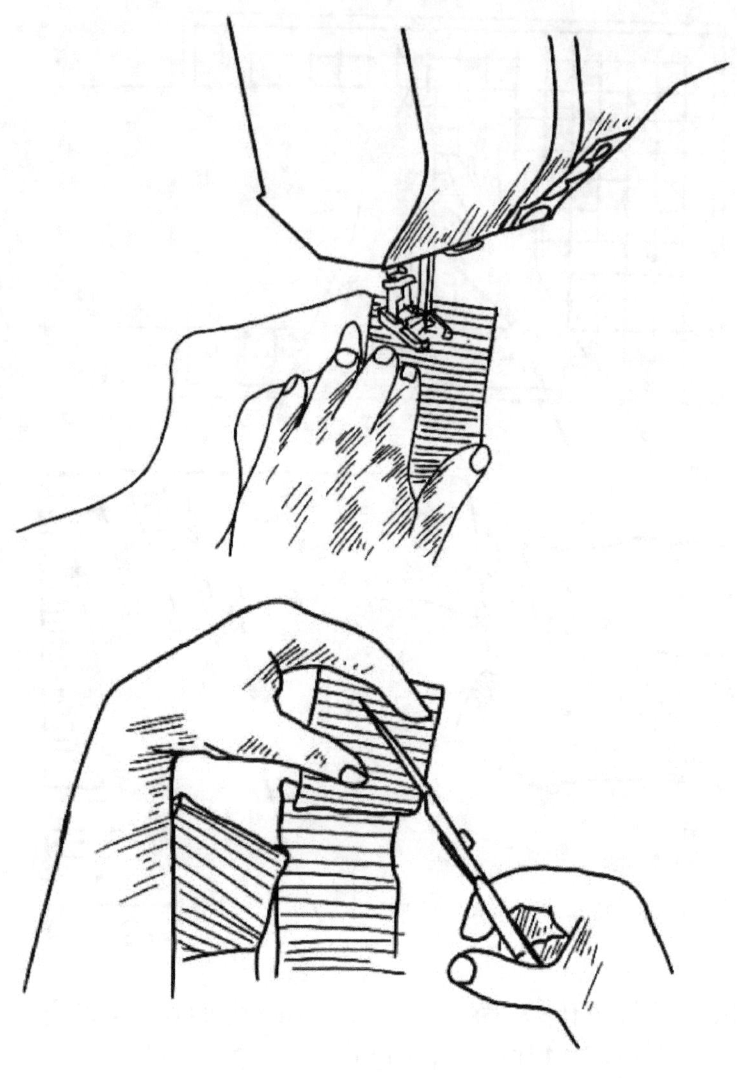

Step 5. Spread your fabric on a surface. Cut a square piece from it. Use the piece as your centerpiece.

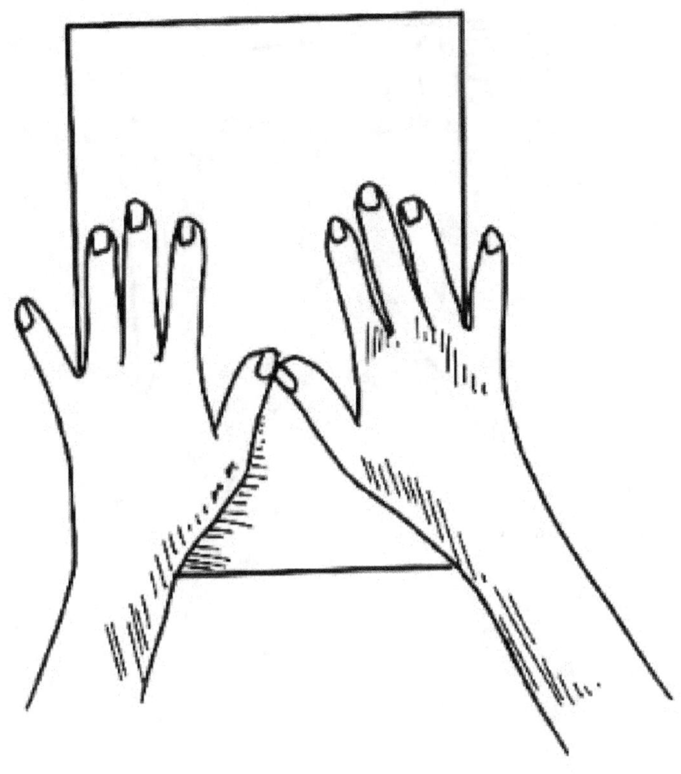

Step 6. Line up the joined strips all over the edges of the center peace. Shape them with the centerpiece to smoothen the quilt.

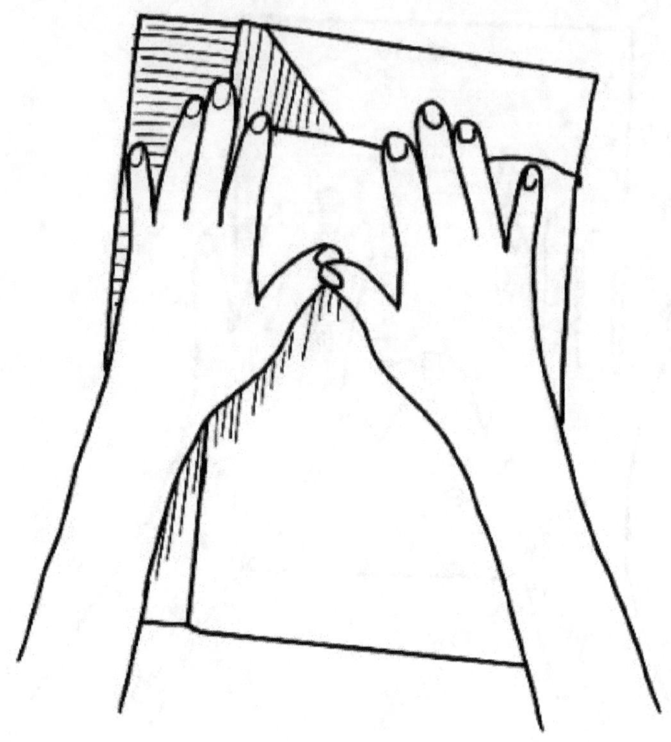

Step 7. Sew the strips together along the edges. Consider using a walking foot if you want better results.

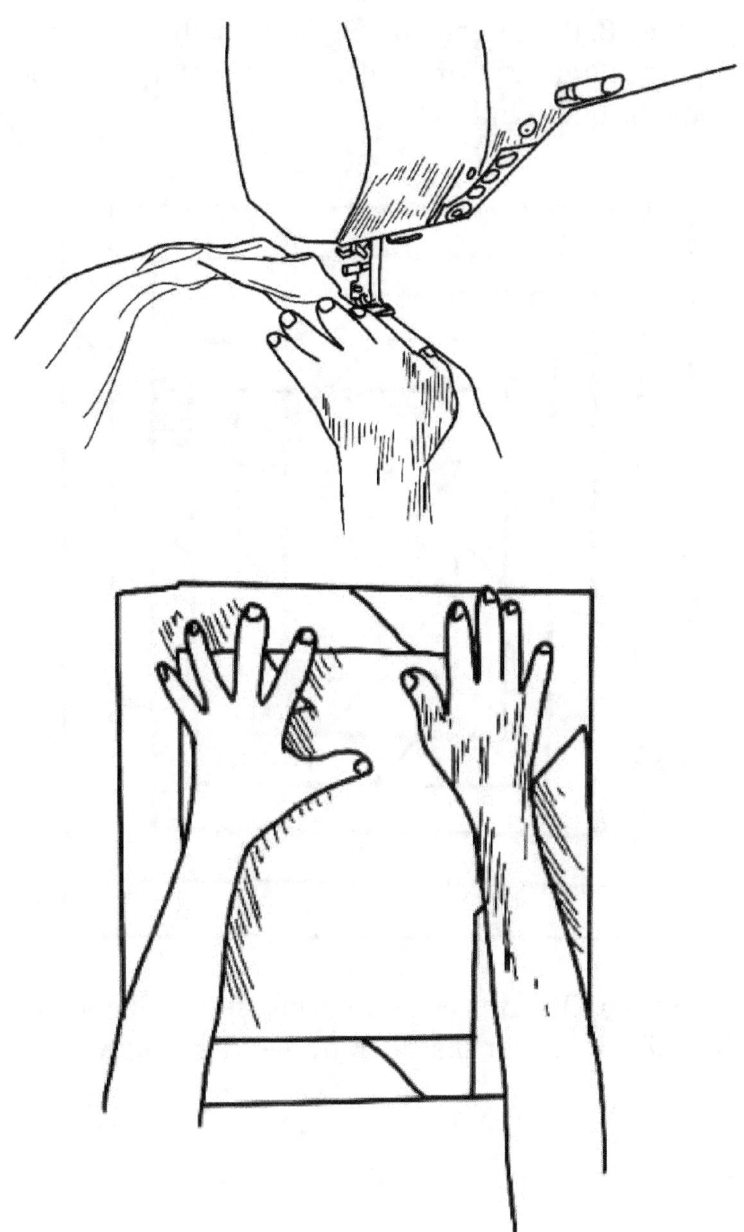

Step 8. Repeat the process continually to get the required number of rings all over the centerpiece, and ready the quilt sandwich.

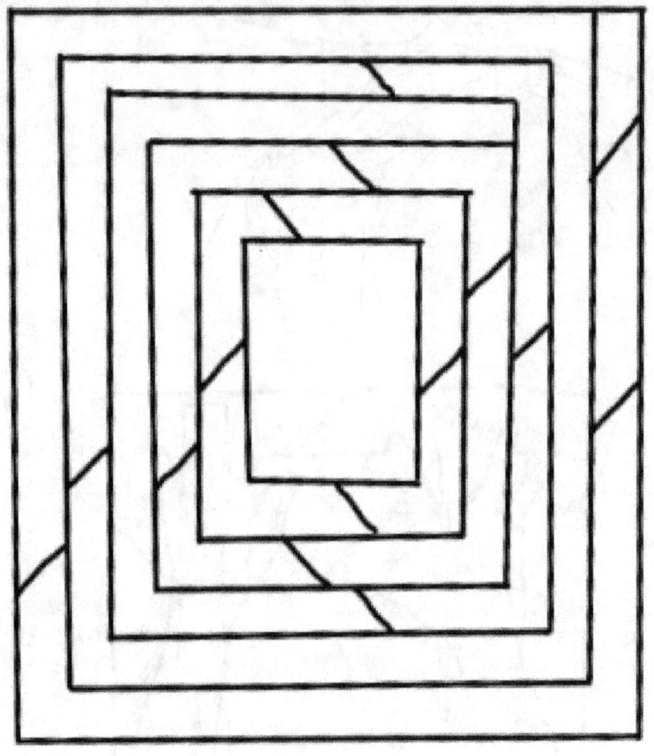

Step 9. Quilt the edges to firmly secure and hold the quilt. Join your shattered frame to the quilt.

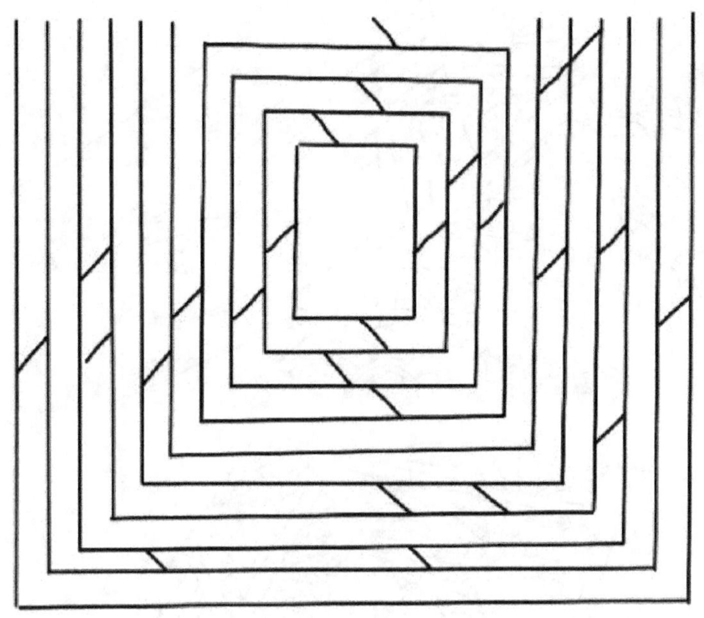

Step 10. Draw additional patterns to fill the negative space. You may download patterns if you can't create one from the scratch.

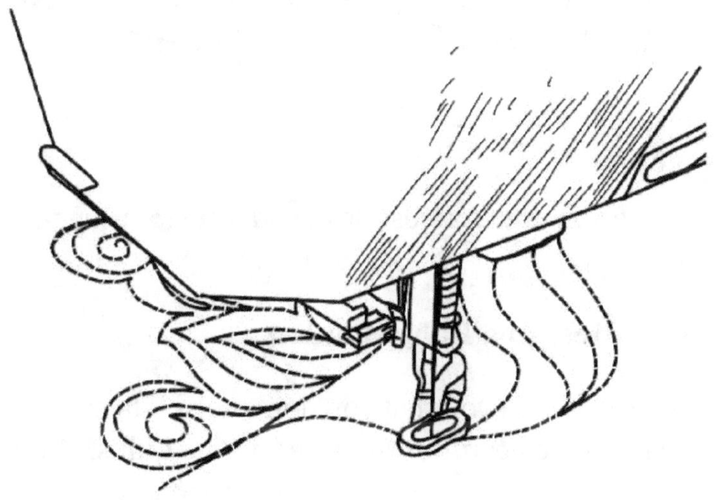

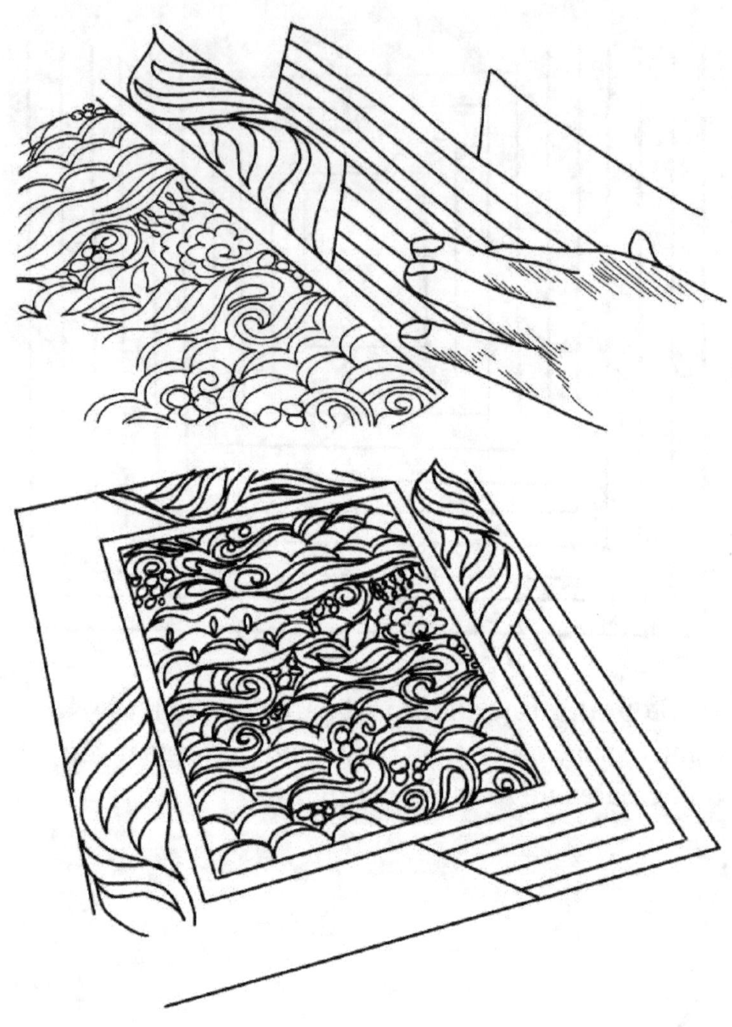

Here you are. You just designed a custom-made quilt.

How to Design a Baby Blanket

I already told you that you don't need lots of fabric to create beautiful shattered-frame quilts. Here is a lovely baby quilt that you can design with just 2 yards of fabric. Yes, creating a well-fitted baby quilt isn't always easy but you'll have no problem getting this right. I will teach you how to design this cute quilt at the comfort of your home. Use any fabric with baby-friendly colors to design this quilt and you'll surely love it. Here's how to design the blanket.

Required Materials

- 36" fabric (panel pink mixed with gold sparkle)

- 36" fabric (little fruit white)

- Thread

- Needle (according to thread)

- A pair of scissors

- 36" high loft batting

- Sewing machine

- Safety pins

Instructions

Follow these simple steps to design your own baby blanket.

Step 1. Spread your fabric on a flat surface and cut the selvage edges. Carefully trim the edges until equal size is attained.

Step 2. Shape the batting to 44" by 36" or the size of your panel. Pin the batting to the wrong side of one fabric before you attach the other fabric, but make sure their right sides stay together.

Step 3. Sew around the edges of the fabric but leave 1/2" for seam allowance. Still, create an opening of about five inches to pull out the right side of the fabric. Just make sure you trim the corners of the blanket before this is done.

Step 4. Flip the right side out through the opening, and press the blanket to straighten the edges. Pin the opening.

Step 5. Stitch the top of the opening to close it. Also sew around the edge of the blanket, leaving out the 1/4" seam allowance.

Step 6. Top-stitch the quilt over the panel boxes to arrange the layers together and attain a more lofty appearance. Do it until the whole thing turns to what you want. Backstitch and cut excess threads.

You just designed your beautiful baby blanket.

How to Create a Crazy Quilt Pattern

Crazy quilts are colorful and fun to design. They are adorable quilts you can design from home with just fabric scraps. Still, with creativity at its peak, you can alter the pattern to make it suitable for your quilt. So, rather than throwing away the scraps of your fabric, use them to design lovely crazy quilts. You don't know how to design a crazy quilt pattern? No worries, that's why I am here.

Required Materials

- Quilting ruler

- Cutting mat

- Rotary cutter

- Thread

- Needle (according to thread)

- A pressing iron and ironing board

- A pair of scissors

- Seam ripper

- Different sizes of fabric scraps

- Muslin

- Sewing machine

Instructions

Follow these simple steps to design your own crazy quilt pattern.

Step 1. Cut one square of muslin for your backing piece to stabilize your quilt block. Feel free to put the batting at the back of the muslin piece if you want to vary the quilt pattern.

A fabric piece at the center of the block will be amazing. Just trim the piece to create room for five different sizes with irregular angles, and roughly position the piece in the center of your backing fabric. Always make sure that the middle piece of your block is different a little bit.

Step 2. Pick the next fabric to attach to the block but make sure that its edges are straight. Still, the edges of the fabric should be as long as the middle piece. Align the edges of the fabric with the first one but make sure that the right side of the second fabric faces down before you sew them together.

Sew on a straight line along the edges, leaving 1/4" seam allowance. Don't stitch unless the first piece is shorter than the second one.

Step 3. Press the seams to ease the process and trim excess threads too. Don't forget your crazy quilt needs lots of pressing, trimming, and sewing. So, let your pressing iron, cutting mat, and iron board stay close to your sewing machine.

Step 4. Add the next pieces of fabric in the center piece left-hand side to properly align them. Just make sure the fabric is long enough to reach the other piece. It is normal for part of the first piece to show. As soon as all is set, sew the pieces together on a straight line across the edge, leaving 1/4" seam allowance.

Step 5. Slightly fold the backing a little bit from the seam and trim the excess edges. Add strips but don't cut them until you have sewn everything together. Extend the pieces across all the angles to add more 'craziness' to the quilt. Just be creative to make the quilt appealing.

Step 6. Remove stitches that do not hold your fabric backing. Use the seam ripper to do it. You won't be able to fold the backing if you fail to cut the stitches. Still, be mindful of how you remove these stitches or you'll rip the seams.

Step 7. Cover the backing piece with strips and trim the edges to balance the square and the backing fabric. Sew the block all over, 1/8" from the edge. Once this is done, sewing the blocks or securing the edges becomes very easy. Add additional blocks and sew everything together.

You just designed your own crazy quilt, congratulations.

How to Design a Snail's Trail Quilt Pattern

Here is a fun and popular quilt pattern that you can design at the comfort of your home. The snail's trail pattern has a few spiral patterns but is hard to create. No worries. With the few tips I want to share with you, nothing can stop you from creating one straight away. Still, feel free to add a few themes and colors to beautify your snail's trail quilt pattern. Here's how to design it.

Instructions

Follow these simple steps to design your own snail's trail quilt pattern.

Step 1. Sew a 1 5/8" by 42" light strip with a 1 5/8" by 42" dark strip, leaving 1/4"seam allowance. Press the seam to the direction of the dark strip and trim either end of the strip to 1 5/8" segment. Add the 1 5/8" leftover strips and sew the two segments together to form a four-patch unit. Place similar colors diagonally on either side and fan your seam allowance if you have bulky patches.

Step 2. Assemble the quilt block. Chain-piece each triangle to quickly assemble your quilt block. Try to master sewing for this project before you try to assemble your block. Still, you need to match your patchwork's midpoint. But, before this can be done, you need to fold your triangles to 2 equal halves. Cut 2 ½" squares, place the squares around the patchwork's four sides, and sew everything together, leaving 1/4" seam allowance. Press the seam allowance to the direction of the triangles.

Add 2 1/2" dark triangles to the edges of the patchwork and press the quilt. Continue to add more triangles until the pattern is perfect for your quilt. Feel free to alternate the sizes of your triangles, from small to large ones. Press your block until it measures 9 1/2" by 9 ½". Sew the block as soon as this is achieved.

Step 3. Arrange blocks in seven rows of six quilt blocks per row. Just make sure that the blocks are carefully aligned in the form of 'O' colors before you attach the quilt blocks.

Step 4. Arrange blocks on each row and sew them together. But don't forget to spread the blocks to opposite directions. You may have to press the quilt carefully to match each seam allowance.

Step 5. Join straight borders with the quilt. Inner borders should be 3 1/2" wide. Use the dark border fabric to cut your border.

Step 6. Press the quilt and use batting and backing to sandwich it. Use a hand or quilting machine to stitch the quilt. Also, cut off excess backing and batting from the edges of your quilt.

How to Design Hugs and Kisses Quilt Pattern

Hugs and Kisses quilt pattern, also known as the X's and O's, is a colorful quilt pattern you'll always want to design. It sits well as a baby quilt or other regular quilts, and it is easy to design. With a well cut-out layout and very nice shapes, you just can't wait to have this lovely quilt on your arms. Again, you're free to alter or vary the size of the quilt, as you want. Just up your level of creativity and create your favorite hugs and kisses quilt pattern. Like other quilters out there, feel free to create the quilt out of pre-cut 5-inches squares, if that works fine for the project you want to design. Also, there are hosts of colors to spice up your design. Any color that works fine for you is great but mix only colors that complement one another. Here's how to design your own hugs and kisses quilt.

Required Materials

- 5" by 5" dark squares (168)

- 2 3/4" by 2 3/4" light squares (336)

- 54" by 63" batting

- 54" by 63" backing

- Sewing machine

- Thread

- Needle (according to thread)

Instructions

Follow these simple steps to design your own hugs and kisses quilt pattern.

Step 1. Sketch a line from one end of a corner to the other till you cover all the small squares, and bring together two light squares and one dark square. Align the right sides of the light and dark squares. Just make sure you lay open their edges. Sew a seam over the line from top-right downward.

Step 2. Sew through every layer, leaving 1/4" seam allowance. Press the right side of the light fabric and the seam to design a triangle. Sew the next light square with the larger dark square's opposite edge. Use the previous strategy or method to do it. Trim the edges to smoothen the quilt pattern.

Step 3. Repeat the process till the 168 dark squares align with opposite sides' light triangles. Arrange all the units in rows and sew everything together.

Step 4. Spread the blocks in seven rows. Each row should have just 6 quilt blocks. Carefully consider the layout of the design to see if you like it. If you don't, just shuffle the blocks, and see how the layout now looks. Sew the blocks together once the layout looks perfect for you.

Step 5. Press all seams flat and carefully join all the rows together, align the seam intersections, and press again.

Step 6. Carefully remove extra batting and backing, and smoothen the edges of the quilt. Double fold the binding and sew on a straight line across the edges.

How to Create Hugs and Kisses quilt with Varied Proportions

Feel free to vary the proportions of your X's and O's quilts. Alternate the larger squares with a few half-sized corner squares to vary your quilts. Just pay keen attention to the materials below if you want to design varied proportions of this lovely and appealing quilt.

Use these materials if you want to design a 36 inches by 45 inches Hugs and kisses quilt for babies.

- Batting and backing (as shown above)

- 5" by 5" dark squares (80)

- 2 1/2" by 2 1/2" light squares (160)

- 77" by 88" bed quilt (11" blocks, larger)

- 6" by 6" squares (224)

- 2 1/2" by 2 1/2" squares (448).

To alter your quilt, just add or subtract the adjustment from the height and width of your blocks. Still, eight small squares or four larger squares need to be added or subtracted, depending on what you really want to achieve. Also, one or more borders will be attached to the quilt.

How to Use Cornerstones and Sashings to Design a Straight Quilt

Sashing, a fabric strip or patchwork, splits one quilt block from the other. Each strip comes with nice squares that beautify the corners and sides of a quilt. Apart from enhancing the aesthetics of your quilt layout, sashing helps frame the quilt blocks, remove poor or unattractive patchworks, boost Quilt's dimensions, and balance blocks of different sizes within the quilt. Cornerstones, like sashings, can make your quilt appealing and attractive. No words can capture the striking effects that sashing and cornerstones will leave on your quilt. Just a few tricks and you'll design this straight quilt right there in your home. Here's the how.

Required Materials

- Fabric

- Thread

- Measuring tools

- Iron

- Sewing machine

- Cutting tools

Instructions

Follow these simple steps to design your straight quilt with sashings and cornerstones.

Step 1. Calculate the dimensions of the cornerstones and sashing to know the size of fabric you need for the project. Also, while deciding the length and width of your sashing, don't use strips that are not suitable for your quilt blocks' dimensions. Measure the width of your block and go for a one-fourth size sashing. In other words, if your quilt block is 12 inches, your sashing should be 3 inches.

Step 2. Sketch your quilt layout to know the amount of sashing strips and cornerstones to use for the project. Also, you need to decide the number of blocks on each row and the total rows of the quilt.

Step 3. Stylishly sew sashing units with the rows of the quilt. But feel free to sew them at the ends of your rows to create a striking effect, leaving 1/4" seam allowance. Press the seams to the direction of your sashing strips, and repeat the process till you assembled all the rows.

Align sashing strip ends with block ends and sew them together if they have equal lengths. But, should the lengths vary, fold the sashing to know its midpoint. Align midpoints and ends, and sew the blocks together to create a few narrow block rows.

Step 4. Press the seam allowance to the direction of the sashing but make sure you don't stretch the narrow rows. Sew every row and align your seam intersections, but don't forget to press the quilt flat.

You just created the straight quilt.

Chapter Summary

- Shattered frame quilts are unique and appealing, and you only need a few strips of fabric to create one.

- A well-fitted baby blanket is a cute quilt for every child you love, and you can easily design it right there in your home.

Next chapter captures Modern X quilt patterns. See you there!

Chapter Eight: Modern X

Quilts' layouts are changing rapidly in order to meet up with the changing demands. What used to be acceptable many years ago is paving way for new designs. Modern X quilts are bold, beautiful, and charming, but difficult to perfect. Still, they are designs you can run from the comfort of your home if you have someone to put you through. Yes, I am here to teach you how to create your own Modern X quilt straight away. Just pay keen attention to these tricks.

Required Materials

- A Plain Textile or Cloth

- A color role of pre-cut Textile or Cloth

- Needle

- Threads

- Rotary cutter

Instructions

Follow these simple steps to design your own Modern X quilt

Step 1: Cut out some shreds from your plain cloth. You will have to incise several hefty squares out of your plain cloth.

Step 2: After, you have to also incise several larger squares. Then incise those larger squares transversely in a triangular form.

Step 3: Afterward, you will constrict some selected pre-cut shreds to 2 breadths. After that, you will have to design a 36 square block using clipped and unclipped shreds

Step 4: Now design 3 sets of shreds with 2 shreds in each set. It is important to make use of plain shreds incised in any one of them

Step 5: Now sew them to design a square of 6 shreds. You have to press them to eject any crumples before you split clothes straight into 2 broad shreds.

Step 6: Design another 2 shreds like that and incise them just like the previous ones. You will organize those shreds, systematically, in couple of 6 shreds

Step 7: Stitch the shreds together to make 36 square boxes. Design another 7 square boxes. Now take 3 shreds from your pre-cut shreds clipped to 2 breadths

Step 8: Assemble them mutually with a balance of 2", sew them together, and build another 2 more of these but this time balance will be in other direction

Step 9: Cut your shed from the verge at 45 degree. Now, design another incise at 45 degree but in the opposite path. Make sure the wider side of the shred is 18 and a quarter in length exactly. Now cut one more out of that shred

How to Design a Straight Line Quilting

Straight line quilting, an amazing quilt design, requires total endurance to create. You may not be able to quilt if you skip every little detail. To achieve straight line quilt, we have made up this simple and speedy step-by-step procedure you can follow. Believe me you will not make any mistake if you can follow it meticulously. Now can we embark on the straight line quilting journey?

Required Materials

- A quilt all sandwiched

- basting

- A walking foot

- A guide bar and tape

- Quilting gloves

- High-quality needles and thread.

Instructions

Follow these simple steps to design your own straight line quilting

Step 1: Create a large room by the left side of the sewing machine to spread out the quilt.

Step 2: Start quilting in the center where there is a joint running down the quilt to allow you stitch in a straight line.

Step 3: Bend the right side of the quilt softly to ease its movement through the sewing machine.

Step 4: Start stitching quilt.

Step 5: You have to stitch the first line straight down to the middle of the quilt. Use the joint in the center as your guide. There is no particular way to stitch, you can either stitch from top cover of the right or left depending on your choice and creativity.

Step 6: Stitch neatly downward until you get to the batting at the base, then cut the thread. Afterward, increase the presser foot and tug the quilt in the direction of the presser foot until it got to the batting at the top again.

Step 7: You should not drag the quilt across the stitching machine. Try to hold the quilt with your hand and weigh the heaviness.

Step 8: Continue threading the quilting lines across the line anyhow you like but make it neat.

Step 9: You should set your guide bar to 1 1/2" away from the needle. After that, stitch from the right side of the guide bar through the left of the sewing line. You should try and skip two lines of the sewing. This will save your time and make it much faster.

Step 10: Carry on your quilting in only one line from top to bottom until you get to the edge of the quilt. The seam lines in your quilt top will help you to maintain a straight line.

Step 11: after you have quilted the line to the middle, move it to the other part of the quilt to finish the rest of the lines from base to summit.

Step 12: Now that you are done quilting, square up the sides, join it, and then you have made an attractive quilt.

Tips for Piercing Curves

Curves are charming. Although they appear complex to build, they are always very simple if only you understand the step by step of designing it. Several designers are frightened by the complexity of the curves but if you are capable of stitching a 1/4" seam. Then fear not, you should be able to stitch a very attractive curve. There is no cause for alarm, with some tips, confidence, endurance and rehearsal, you should sketch and stitch a nice curve. Now, let's try out some tips needed to stitch beautiful piercing curves.

Required Materials

- Cloth

- Rotary cutter

- A pair of scissors

- A guide bar and tape

- Sewing Machine

- Needles and thread.

Instructions

Follow these simple steps to pierce the curves.

Step 1: Thicken your cloth before cutting. The starch will not allow the sides from becoming threadbare or worn-out. It is advisable to use old plain starch on your cloth. This will make it more strong and durable.

Step 2. You should be careful with the type of prototype you follow and cut. Using a precise prototype can help you to achieve good results. It is advisable you use a rotary cutter for the straight lines and paper scissors for the curves. However, if achieving precision is your issue, it is better you contemplate picking a design with corresponding acrylic templates.

Step 3: you have to thread slowly when trimming your cloth or textile especially those one gotten from plastic models or straight from acrylic templates. But remember that you should be careful with the way you trace it. Take it gently.

You want to be as accurate as possible since you will be using the curved cut raw edges as a guide for your scant 1/4" seam. You will cut more accurate pieces when using a combination of sharp fabric scissors and a small 28mm rotary cutter. Try both and see what works best for you!

Step 4: Pin your curves. Pinning is tasking and time consuming, but the time is actually worth it if you are able to pin it neatly. To pin, you can take a convex and concave piece and spot the middle of both curved sides by bending them in the middle, unbend and place a pin at the crinkles. After this, bend the base and the upper sides to contact the middle pin, make the edges ranged, unbend and place pins at the crinkles.

Step 5: After you might have placed the marking pin, locate and pin the middle marks of curve pieces mutually. Also, you must increase pins in between to save the raw ends range. This pinning system is cumbersome but you should exercise patience, and confidence to understand it.

Step 6: Stitch gently. It is advisable you do a stop and start method while sewing. You have to stitch the curves slowly and be very sure that the raw ends remain united as you go ahead with the stitch. Make sure you stop and fine-tune the cloth to eschew wrinkles. Also, try to always halt with the needle in the extreme position in order to make your extension stay put on the machine. Employ a ¼ foot presser to get the perfect seam allowance.

Step 7: Stitch with your bowl-shaped piece on top. Avoid crumples. You should endeavour to stop often and use your finger to make sure your levels are laying flat in the capacity you are about to stitch.

How to Make a Modern Barn Quilt

Here is the colourful modern barn quilt. It is charming, gorgeous, appealing, fitting, and you can surely design it from home. Just a few tricks and you're on the way creating your own modern barn quilt.

Required Materials

- Plywood

- Lumber

- Stain

- (50) 1-1/4" exterior screws

- Paint samples

- Painter's tape

- (6) 5" bolts

- 2" by 8" board

Instructions

Follow these simple steps to design own modern barn quilt

Step 1. Select Your Design and Buy Paint: In order to make a unique barn quilt, you must have a good knowledge of color. You should be able to use a refreshing and bright color palette that will help to achieve the aim of the work.

Use corresponding paint colors to the palette to be designed. Most of the producers of the paints have developed software that will assist you to get colors that match your project without considering the line of colors.

Step 2. Select and Cut Lumber: You must know that the magnitude of the barn quilt you are creating before you select the lumber. Just know that most barn quilts customarily have eight-foot squares, with small space available in the barn.

You must scale it down in order to build your quilt with a 4 by 4 piece of 1/4 plywood base, and planned 1 by 8 pine boards. Prior to cutting the plywood, make sure to dry the pine boards together, and quantify to know that the quilt could be a 50 square. I cut all boards to that length.

Step 3. Stain and Assemble: Staining is mandatory, infact, leaving your board natural is better. This allows you to test if your board can pass the test of time. Although, there is no problem if you decide to paint yours. However, if you want to stain make it transparent enough so that the grain of the wood will appear through it. After drying up your stain, turn the board over and place it on a square and put a 4 by 4 plywood on it.

Screw the plywood and the board but try as much as possible to make sure that the position of the board is maintained. You can put between 6 to 8 screws on the plywood and boards. Also, when staining your board, make sure all the ends at being painted and the sides of the 4 by 4 plywood especially those areas that are visible

Step 4. Plan for Painting: You can use any color of choice to paint as long as it will make your design look attractive. To paint there is a need for you to have a tape and expertly know how to Mark a line through a pencil, ruler and long straight material such as play wood.

Step 5. Paint the Design: The process of painting may actually span through some days, but if you actually dedicate time with some level of endurance you can mark it happening in just one day. You can make your painting look simple and easy but masking your tape with your pencil lines in several locations of your designs. At the same time, make use of varieties of colors.

Close to the end of the painting, you must slow down and allow one color to dry up before taping the next part. This is because there is not enough space again and if you do not exercise patience, you will end up making a mistake. You know that 2-3 coats of paint are needed in each space. The outdoor painting is easy because the air flow will dry it up quickly.

Get happy with your art and display it openly. You must determine where to display it by drilling the barn close to your target stud and place your quilt with a board already installed as a ledger. This ledger forms a sit when attaching the bolts.Once you place your quilt, use two bolts on the head and at the base of the quilt barn. At this time, remove the sit, and step a little bit backward to cross check your artwork, and appreciate it.

How to Create a Framed Barn Quilt

A framed barn quilt is beautiful and colorful, just like other great quilts you already learn to design in this book. Still, it is one quilt you can design from home for someone who probably means the world to you. Here's is how to create the quilt.

Required Materials

- Drill

- Exterior-grade screws

- Measuring tape and straight edge

- Paint, paintbrushes and a roller

- Painter's tape

- Circular saw

- D-rings and picture hanging wire

- One 4" x 8" x 3/4" sheet of plywood

- Two 1" x 4" x 8" frame

- Two 1" x 3" x 8" mat

- wood putty

- Pattern template

- Wood stain

- Pneumatic staple gun and staples

Instructions

Follow these simple steps to design your own framed barn quilt.

Step 1: Cut Plywood to Size: The Art is customarily a square. To begin, use a 4" by 8" sheet of plywood. Reduce it to appropriate size to contain the available space.

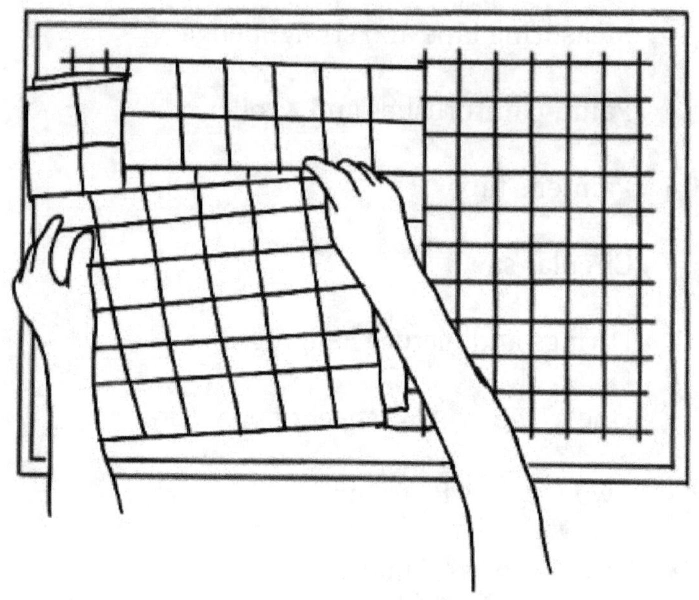

Step 2: Lay Out Design: Employ a vertical edge to mark out your project. Your design should have a square that is splitted into four triangles each. It is important to leave space of about two and half borders by the side of all your design to make it 1 by 3 wood matte. This will allow it to sit comfortably on the top of the canvas. You should try and slightly Mark each triangle with a colored pencil you intend to paint with to avoid mistakes.

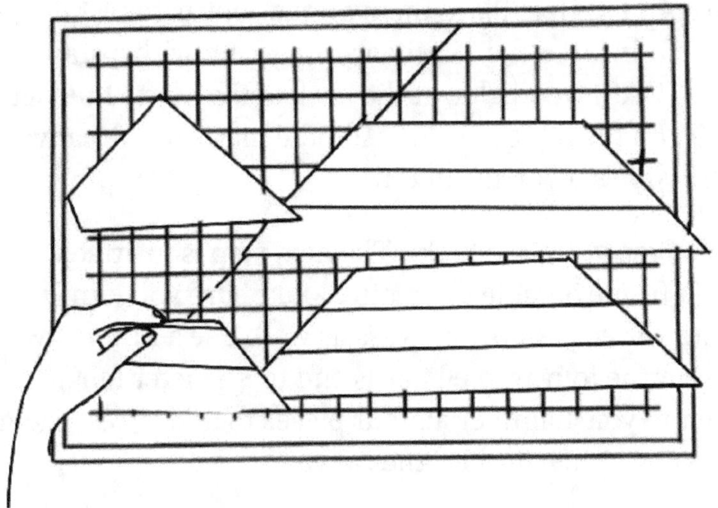

Step 4: Employ a tape to indicate all the sections for your slightest color. Make your paint start from the lightest color to deepest color. This will allow you to detect any mistake easily and mask it out. Put Paint on sections you have already taped-off. After this remove the tape from a 45-degree angle before the paint is dried up in order to have a clean side of the project.

Step 5: Tape and Paint Second Color: Now you are done with the first painting. Remove the tape from the lines in order to apply the next color. Maintain the same pattern used in the previous painting until you have successfully completed the painting of all sections.

Step 6: Add a Matte: A matte of 1" by 3" size should be cut to the angle of the canvas with 45-degree mitered corners. You should use a miter saw to cut this edge. Place them on the canvas to test if it will fit in. Join the four boards together with a staple gun. Use a wood glue at the back of the matte then let it lie on the top of the art. Add the matte to the canvas. Drill holes if you deem it fit.

Step 7: Frame It Up: The next step is to attach a 1 by 4 frame outside the matte. Make sure you join it with the edge of the canvass as well. Use a Miter saw to cut the four frame boards end to 42 meter long. Before you hammer all four pieces together, test them to know if they fit into the canvas.

Do another painting here in a desirous way. Join all four pieces together at the corners. Place your frame near the canvas and hammer it to the canvas and matte with screws from the outside edges.

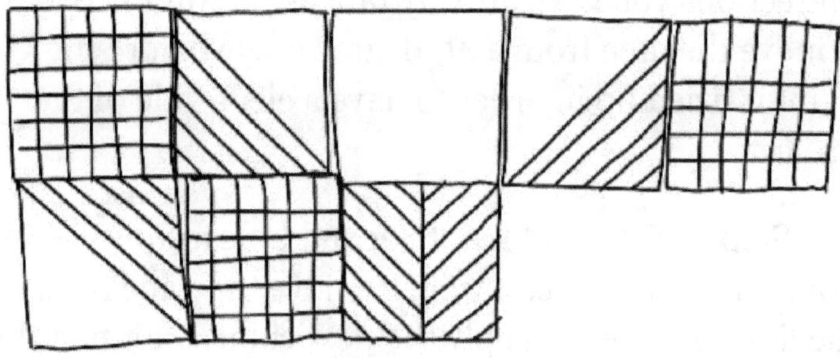

Step 8: Add Hanging Hardware: Add two rings with D patterns to the base of the board and securely insert a wrapping wire around the D-rings for a strong hold. Then hang your design for enjoyment.

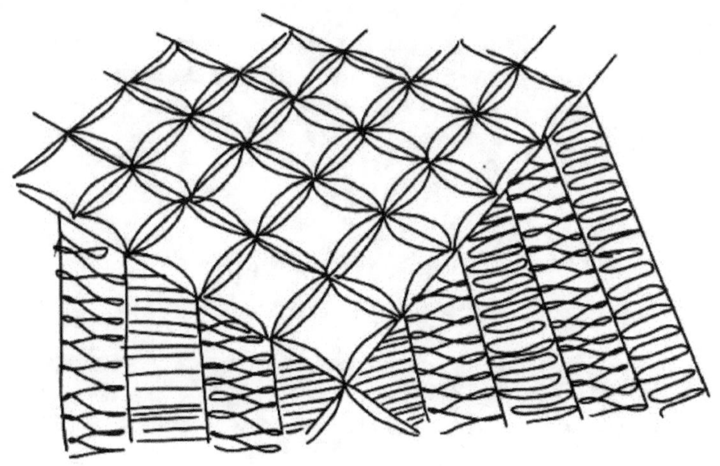

Chapter Summary

- Modern X quilts are bold, beautiful and charming but difficult to design.

- To create one, you need a bit of commitment and creativity.